SOURCE

Fay Sweet

SOURCE

an internet directory of modern interior design

QUADRILLE

CONTENTS

This book was inspired by curiosity. Whenever I look at pictures of amazing interiors, I want to know where the sofa came from, and the taps, and how they got the floor to look like that? I also like to know how the architect created a new space or improved what was already there. I am not alone in my curiosity, so I have compiled this book to explore what goes into making interesting, comfortable and liveable contemporary interiors.

At the heart of *Source* is a collection of inspiring homes from around the world. I never cease to be impressed by the skills of

start to construct a picture in your mind of how the space will be used and how it will look. Whether you choose to hire a professional or not, it helps to have ideas about finishes and furnishings. Finding the perfect leather sofa or dining table can be a real pleasure, but it's not just the big items that count. A beautiful door will be spoiled by a miserable uncomfortable handle. These details not only build character, they will also contribute to your enjoyment of a room.

In the choice of interior shots for *Source*, the emphasis is on a contemporary

pieces are licensed to be made by just one manufacturer, however, where the copyright has expired, they may be produced by a number of companies. The websites provided are either those of the sole manufacturer or one of the companies acknowledged to be making the best quality versions of the design. Beware of opting for the cheapest lookalike products, you usually get what you pay for. There are of course copycat companies at work throughout the furnishing industry, but in the case of more recent designs by the likes of today's

INTRODUCTION

architects, particularly their ability for 3D thinking, in fashioning new spaces as well as remodelling existing rooms; many are expert at the finishes and are fastidious over detail, with an encyclopaedic knowledge of materials and products. Interior designers share many of these skills and possess impressive abilities in building colour schemes, combining textures and sourcing furnishings. *Source* is a window onto this world.

Whether your aim is to transform a room or build a house from scratch, you'll

style of home with modern classic furniture and lighting, together with shelving and storage, items for kitchens, bathrooms, bedrooms and gardens and details right down to the light switches. In recent years, coinciding with our desire to live in open-plan, uncluttered, stylish homes, there has been a growing interest in classic designs by the great Modernist heroes, including Le Corbusier, Ludwig Mies van der Rohe, and Charles and Ray Eames; many of their greatest designs are featured here. In some cases, these classic

stars such as Philippe Starck, Marc Newson and Jasper Morrison the manufacturers given here will be the sole producers of the genuine article.

As we all become more aware of the importance and pleasures of comfortable, good-looking and practical interiors, we have become design aficionados. With the comprehensive range of products on show throughout the book, *Source* is designed to make it quicker and easier to track down exactly what you are looking for.

How to use Source

Source provides maximum inspiration and information for anyone interested in design. The book's layout is unique – opposite every page showing a stunning interior, there is a page of products chosen either because they have stood the test of time and are widely recognised modern design classics or because they have the potential to become classics of the future.

In the case studies, architects and designers outline their ideas for each project, along with any necessary problem solving en route, and together with the clients, describe as many items as possible in the rooms. In the place of captions, pictures are annotated with descriptions of the products and the website of their manufacturer. Where the provenance of an item is uncertain, manufacturers of similar items are suggested.

Source is absolutely a book of its time. With an increasing number of us using the worldwide web as a research and communication tool, *Source* gives web addresses to make it easy to find designers, manufacturers and suppliers.

In the case of the architect or designer, by visiting their website, you'll be gaining access to their portfolio of work. If you are undertaking a major project, this is a fascinating way of building a shortlist of people who might be right for the job.

Increasingly, architects and designers are finding that their clients are using the web to make their choice – their websites are usually very good.

When it comes to the manufacturers, the majority of those named in *Source* export their products around the world. Almost without exception, the quality of the website designs and the level of information available is astonishingly good. This is a huge, valuable and under-sung resource. Most sites are very good looking and easy to navigate, many have information giving the materials and dimensions of the product and the range of finishes available. Together with looking at the range of products, it's possible to find out about the company's history, its design philosophy, information about the designers and details of your nearest stockist.

• *Source* is designed to help you find the very best of modern design for the home; it provides a link with manufacturers who can guide you to your nearest retailer

• once you have found an item you like, enter the manufacturer's website address into your computer

• in many cases the manufacturer's central website is listed, but there may be national and regional options too

• after entering the manufacturer's website, you'll find a world of information; many not only have details of the full range of products, they also carry information about designers, along with the technical specifications, materials and dimensions of the products

• should you encounter any problems activating a website address, it is a good idea, as an alternative, to type the manufacturer's name into a search engine

• some manufacturers do not show their entire collection on the website, but in many cases it is possible to order a brochure of the full range of goods

• if you decide to buy a particular item, many websites have a section which lists the main importers and distributors for different countries; these can be contacted to find your nearest stockist

• where the importers and distributors are not included, go to the manufacturer's contact info and send an email stating the product you'd likeand your town or city and ask for your nearest retailer

• in those cases where a retailer is not nearby, use the email facility to ask the manufacturer for information about shipping the product direct to your home

- comfortable seating is a must: the sofa is the key item, but take care to keep it in scale with the room as they can take up a huge amount of space

- there's plenty of scope for interesting lighting: don't just rely on a central pendant lamp, table and floor lamps add variety and flexibility

- a fireplace is unnecessary with central heating, but wonderful; many gas fires are excellent, but a real fire is hard to beat

- coffee tables or side tables are extremely useful for cups and glasses

- dimmer switches quickly change the lighting levels; programmable lighting systems are an increasingly affordable luxury

- as living rooms are used so intensively, good storage, whether cupboards, shelving or a mixture of the two, makes it easier to tidy away books, music CDs, videos and DVDs

The living room is one of the most intensively used spaces in the home: it has to be flexible and adaptable throughout the day, from catching up with the breakfast news to evening dining or entertaining. Above all, this is a place to rest, away from outside pressures, so comfortable seating is an essential component. The sofa will be a

facing each other feels like a waiting room, an L-shaped configuration is more social and makes it easy for people to talk together. Where space is at a premium, choose a smaller scale sofa and a couple of armchairs. Additional seating can be provided with an upholstered bench or side chairs. Lighting is an important

LIVING ROOMS

major purchase and set the tone of the room – a sleek black leather and chrome design has a metropolitan look, corduroy or colourful plain wool upholstery is smart and welcoming, stripes can be upbeat, while a floral pattern usually has a country feel. The arrangement of seating is crucial to the way the space is used – two sofas

element in the living room, too. Because it has to cope with so many different uses, it is a good idea to combine pendant lamps with floor, wall and table lamps. Dimmer switches are a great idea, enabling a quick change of tempo. For real luxury, opt for a programmable system where different settings produce different moods

Model No. PK31 (1958) by Poul Kjærholm
□ **www.fritzhansen.com**

Breuer Sofa (1936) by Marcel Breuer
□ **www.isokonplus.com**

Model No. hm991i (1998) by David Chipperfield
□ **www.hitchmylius.com**

Club sofa (1962) by Robin Day
□ **www.loftonline.net**

Milano (1982) by Gionatan De Pas, Donato D'Urbino & Paolo Lomazzi
□ **www.zanotta.it**

Model No. 2213 (1962) by Børge Mogensen
□ **www.fredericia.com**

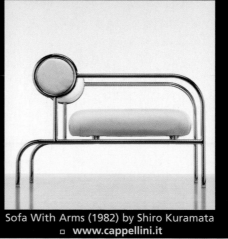

Sofa With Arms (1982) by Shiro Kuramata
□ **www.cappellini.it**

Tolomeo floor lamp in aluminium (1987), Michele de Lucchi & Giancarlo Fassina □ **www.artemide.com**

Superellipse Table in maple (1968), Piet Hein & Bruno Mathsson □ **www.fritzhansen.com**

DKR-2 (Dining Bikini Rod) chair in brown leather (1951), Charles & Ray Eames □ **www.vitra.com**

Met modular sofa in brown leather (1996), Piero Lissoni with S. Sook Kim □ **www.cassina.it**

Party space
by Feeny Mallindine Architects
www.feenymallindine.com

The sociable owners of this Edwardian house love to give parties and even enjoy small musical concerts at home. To make a space for around 30–40 guests, the architect has merged two rooms at the back of the house and added a 2m-deep, sheer glass garden extension across the entire width of the building. The back wall of the house is supported by a single sturdy steel column. The new space is not just perfect for parties, it has the feel of a large apartment and yet is comfortable for the couple when they are alone.

1 Sheer, floor-to-ceiling doors form the front of this capacious bespoke storage wall. The wood used is sycamore, which has been given a tough clear lacquer finish □ **for wood panelling, see the Directory of Suppliers on pages 152–55**

2 The glass used here is a low-emissivity product, which helps to control the temperature of the room. It is used in sealed panels of 8mm glass, with an 8mm air gap and then 10mm glass on the outside. The sliding door is anodised aluminium □ **for architectural glass, see the Directory of Suppliers on pages 152–55**

3 The clients were keen to have a built-in fish tank. This one is unusual because it contains salt water, which supports a great variety of fish. Salt water tanks are slightly more expensive to set up and run than their plain water counterparts □ **for aquariums and fish tanks, see the Directory of Suppliers on pages 152–55**

4 The main part of the room has an American elm floor, with Portuguese limestone in the new glass extension. The honey colour of the elm sits well with the sycamore-faced cupboards □ **for wood and stone flooring, see the Directory of Suppliers on pages 152–55** □ The elm flooring is treated with BonaKemi, a durable water-based sealant that gives the timber a natural finish □ **www.bona.com**

5 Apta Collection, Model No. 9614 coffee table by Antonio Citterio. Shown here with a wenge table top, but is also available in grey oak, brown oak and grey and brown oak with a pickled finish □ **www.maxalto.it**

Lansdowne (2003) by Terence Woodgate
□ **www.scp.co.uk**

Zurigo (1998) by Alfredo Häberli &
Christophe Marchand □ **www.zanotta.it**

Soft Mellow (2002) by Marcel Wanders
□ **www.moooi.com**

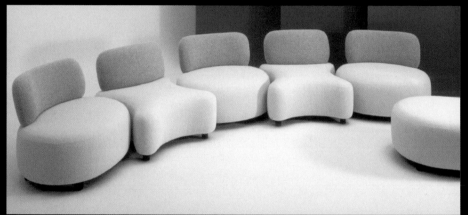

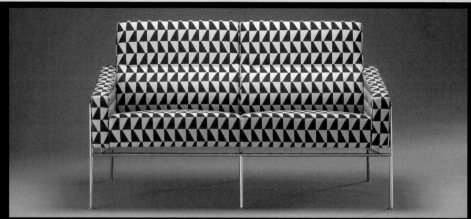

Model No. hm61 (1998) by Nigel Coates
□ **www.hitchmylius.com**

Series 3300, Model No. 3302 (1956) by Arne Jacobsen
□ **www.fritzhansen.com**

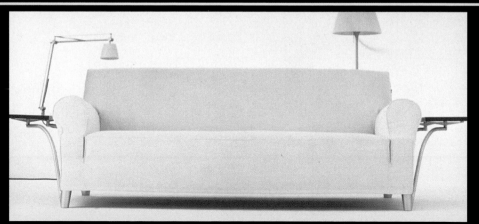

Model No. 3321, Swan Sofa (1958) by Arne Jacobsen
□ **www.fritzhansen.com**

Lazy Working Sofa (1998) by Philippe Starck
□ **www.cassina.it**

606 Universal Shelving System (1960), Dieter Rams □ **www.vitsoe.com**

Parentesi suspended lamp (1970), Achille Castiglioni & Pio Manzu □ **www.flos.net**

Bauhaus lamp (1924), Wilhelm Wagenfeld □ **www.tecnolumen.de**

Model No. PK22 easy chair in natural leather (1955–56), Poul Kjærholm □ **www.fritzhansen.com**

Charles sofa with cream cloth upholstery (1998), Antonio Citterio □ **www.bebitalia.it**

Scandinavian cool

by Shideh Shaygan

www.shaygan.com

When the owners first saw this apartment in an 1880s mansion block, it was dark and cluttered, but they could see the appeal of its large reception rooms. The refurbishment project involved stripping the rooms back to the bare walls, retaining as much of the fine detailing as possible, including the wood panelling and classic Scandinavian fireplace – the kakelugn – and installing new services. The grand architectural scale of the place is now the backdrop to a more contemporary style of living.

1 Original ceramic tiled fireplace, kakelugn, with decorative panels showing hand painted water lilies □ **for architectural salvage, including fireplaces, see the Directory of Suppliers on pages 152–55**

2 BeoSound 3000 music system □ **www.bang-olufsen.com**

3 Block lamp (1996) by Harri Koskinen □ **www.designhouse2.com**

4 Coffee table designed by the architect. Constructed from white oiled oak, this unusual design incorporates built-in lighting □ **www.shaygan.com**

5 Thought to be a Danish design from the 1950s, the interlocking blonde wood tables were found in a Copenhagen second-hand shop □ **for vintage furniture, see the Directory of Suppliers on pages 152–55**

6 Teardrop table lamp (1999) by Anish Kapoor sits on the Danish side tables. This limited edition lamp by the renowned British artist was part of a specially commissioned series of domestic products by sculptors created in conjunction with the Tate Gallery □ **www.homebase.co.uk**

7 The original herringbone-pattern oak parquet had become very dark with age and wear, but has now been sanded and treated with a natural linseed oil mixed with white pigment for a light finish □ **www.triptrap.com**

8 Fields rug by Thomas Eriksson. Hundred-percent wool rug available in various sizes and combinations of 17 colours □ **www.kasthall.se**

9 Painting from the 'Walker' series (2001) by well-known contemporary Swedish artist Jan Håfström □ **www.the-artists.org**

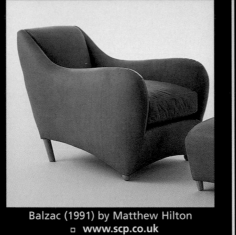

Balzac (1991) by Matthew Hilton
□ **www.scp.co.uk**

Genni (1935) by Gabriele Mucchi
□ **www.zanotta.it**

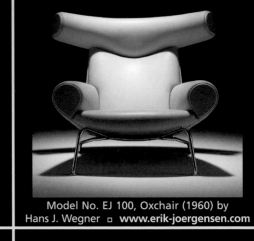

Model No. EJ 100, Oxchair (1960) by
Hans J. Wegner □ **www.erik-joergensen.com**

Model No. EJ 96, Apollo by Foersom &
Hiort-Lorenzen □ **www.erik-joergensen.com**

Armchair 400 (1935–36) by Alvar Aalto
□ **www.artek.fi**

Club by Matthew Hilton
□ **www.scp.co.uk**

Sax (2002) by Terence Woodgate
□ **www.scp.co.uk**

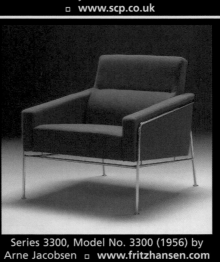

Series 3300, Model No. 3300 (1956) by
Arne Jacobsen □ **www.fritzhansen.com**

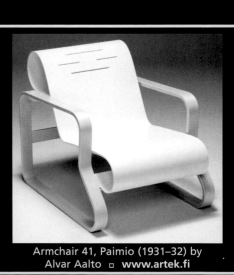

Armchair 41, Paimio (1931–32) by
Alvar Aalto □ **www.artek.fi**

Classic 86 cast iron wood-burning stove (1970) by Bent Falk □ **www.rais.dk**

Series 3300 sofa in black leather (1956), Arne Jacobsen □ **www.fritzhansen.com**

Tolomeo floor lamp in aluminium (1987), Michele de Lucchi & Giancarlo Fassina □ **www.artemide.com**

Model No. PK22 easy chair in black leather (1955–56), Poul Kjærholm □ **www.fritzhansen.com**

Tea Trolley 901 in birch with white laminate (1935–36), Alvar Aalto □ **www.artek.fi**

Delight in the detail
by Smith-Miller + Hawkinson Architects

www.smharch.com

The architect of this house described the design idea bluntly as 'a shipping container on stilts'. This is to severely downplay the elegance of the project. The timber-clad, near-rectangular building is constructed on the side of a sloping valley and stretches out into the landscape on stilts. The full wall of glass at the far end of the living room gives spectacular valley and river views. The 100 square metres of interior space is divided between this open-plan living room with kitchen space, and then beyond are two bedrooms and a bathroom. Whilst appearing a very simple structure, the attention to detail throughout is impressive.

1 Oversized floorlamp. Similar in design to the Fortuny floorlamp by Mariano Fortuny Y Madrazo for Pallucco Italia, designed originally for use in theatres. Available with a black or titanium coloured epoxy powder-coated base with either a black or beige lampshade □ **www.palluccobellato.it**

2 LC1 chair (1928) by Le Corbusier. A chromed tubular steel frame with leather seat and back and slung leather arms □ **www.cassina.it**

3 Oak flooring, coated with a matt sealant □ **for wood flooring, see the Directory of Suppliers on pages 152–55**

4 3107 chair (1955), one of the Series 7 designs, by Arne Jacobsen. One of the most widely imitated contemporary chair designs, which has been in continuous production since the 1950s □ **www.fritzhansen.com**

5 Valmarana dining table in ash (1971) by Carlo Scarpa, now discontinued. Other designs by Carlo Scarpa available from Bernini □ **www.bernini.it**

Model No. 890 (2002) by Liévore, Altherr & Molina ❑ **www.thonet.de**

LC2 Petit Confort (1928) by Le Corbusier, Jeanneret & Perriand ❑ **www.cassina.it**

Model No. 635, Red/Blue Chair (1918) by Gerrit Thomas Rietveld ❑ **www.cassina.it**

Boxer by Ola Rune
❑ **www.skandiform.com**

Ondina (1987) by De Pas, D'Urbino & Lomazzi ❑ **www.zanotta.it**

Breuer Armchair (1936) by Marcel Breuer
❑ **www.isokonplus.com**

Zurigo (1998) by Alfredo Häberli & Christophe Marchand ❑ **www.zanotta.it**

Model No. CH22 (1950) by Hans J. Wegner
❑ **www.carlhansen.com**

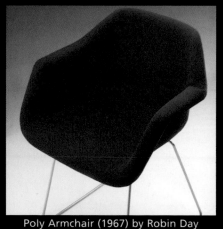

Poly Armchair (1967) by Robin Day
❑ **www.loftonline.net**

Jetmaster Universal 1200 fireplace
□ www.jetmaster.com

Armchair 402 in birch with zebra fabric (1932–33),
Alvar Aalto □ www.artek.fi

Closer to nature
by George Elphick at Elphick Proome Architects

www.eparch.co.za

This large, open, glass-walled extension has been added to the existing structure of the architect's own family home to enhance the connection between the interior and the stunning landscape. The strong relationship with nature is important to the household, especially since the architect's wife runs a natural health practice from home. In addition to this living space, a contrasting cosy study-music room was added, along with a gallery area. The new living space extends into the garden with the addition of the verandah, which is shaded by the protecting 'wing' of the steel-frame roof that swoops upwards towards the forest.

1 Manila chair in polished aluminium by Amat-3. This design is ideal for use outside because it can easily withstand rain and will not rust
□ www.amat-3.com

2 Zen Table in iroko wood by Empire Design. Also available in natural ash and stained ash □ www.empire-design.co.za

3 Le Cube two-seater sofa in black leather and chrome tubular steel by Pago. Also available as a single seater and three seater
□ www.pago.co.za

4 Coffee table on castors designed by the architect and home owner
□ www.eparch.co.za □ Manufactured by Exotic Furniture
□ www.exoticfurniture.co.za

5 In contrast to the balau timber decking outside, the floor is a charcoal oxide-dyed, steel-trowelled screed floor with two-part polyurethane gloss □ for concrete flooring, see the Directory of Suppliers on pages 152–55 □ Cement Floorcote oxide and sealant by Earthcote □ www.earthcote.co.za

6 Burnt-orange wool rug. Similar to Fasett rug in orange 107–1007 from Kasthall □ www.kasthall.se

Model No. PK22 (1955–56) by
Poul Kjærholm ▫ **www.fritzhansen.com**

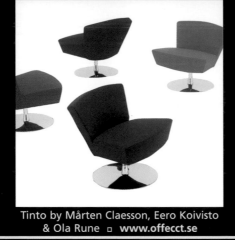

Tinto by Mårten Claesson, Eero Koivisto
& Ola Rune ▫ **www.offecct.se**

Coconut (1955) by George Nelson
▫ **www.vitra.com**

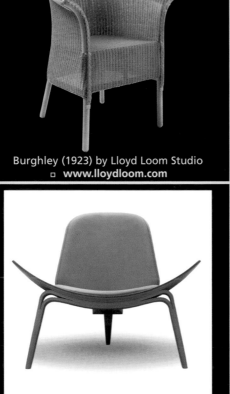

Burghley (1923) by Lloyd Loom Studio
▫ **www.lloydloom.com**

Model No. S35R (1929) by Marcel Breuer
▫ **www.thonet.de**

Mono by Ola Rune
▫ **www.offecct.se**

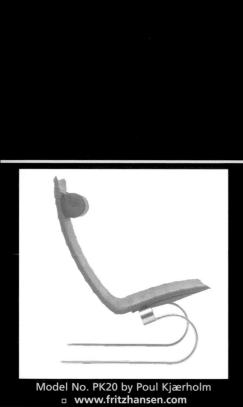

Model No. PK20 by Poul Kjærholm
▫ **www.fritzhansen.com**

Model No. CH07 (1963) by Hans J. Wegner
▫ **www.carlhansen.com**

Clea (1997) by Kristiina Lassus
▫ **www.zanotta.it**

BD:6 chair (1998), Björn Dahlström
▫ **www.cbidesign.se**

Diamond easy chair (1950–52),
Harry Bertoia ▫ **www.knollint.com**

Garden pavilion
by Anna von Schewen Design and Architecture

www.annavonschewen.com

When Anna von Schewen was asked by her brother to create a new family home, her approach was to work from the inside out and focus on the way the house would be used. It naturally divided into three zones – a place for sleeping, a place for cooking and a living/dining room for sharing meals with friends and enjoying the views and nature. The designer's approach is the same when creating furniture where she starts with the body. The living area is a family and entertaining space, wood clad on two walls and the upward sloping ceiling, with two walls of floor-to-ceiling glass. The large expanses of glass

allow the room to stand almost like an open pavilion. The transparency of the space gives the family the close contact it wants with the surrounding landscape. The house has water on both sides and at certain times of day, the sloping ceiling picks up animated reflections.

1 Latta easy chair (1997) by Anna von Schewen. This unusual chair is built with strips of sensuously curved laminated wood and covered with a woven fabric so the whole chair bends and moulds itself to the shape of the body ▫ **www.annavonschewen.com**

2 Walls and ceiling are clad in vertical timber boarding, which encourages the eye upwards and makes the space appear to soar. The boards add an interesting and subtle texture to the space and are painted white to keep the room feeling open and fresh ▫ **for wood cladding, see the Directory of Suppliers on pages 152–55**

3 Bespoke dining table designed and made by the architect ▫ **www.annavonschewen.com**

4 Like most of this structure, the floor is made from pine that has been given a light coat of whitewash ▫ **for wood flooring, see the Directory of Suppliers on pages 152–55**

5 EJ 220 sofa, designed and produced by Erik Jørgensen ▫ **www.erik-joergensen.com**

6 Regnbågsmattan striped rug, designed by Josef Frank ▫ **www.svenskttenn.se**

Model No. 3316, The Egg with footstool (1958) by
Arne Jacobsen □ **www.fritzhansen.com**

Model No. EJ 5, Corona (1961) by Poul Volther
□ **www.erik-joergensen.com**

Tipto (2004) by Peter Emerys-Roberts & Christine Harvey
□ **www.driade.com**

Model No. S411 (1932) by Thonet
□ **www.thonet.de**

Scoop (2000) by Mårten Claesson, Eero Koivisto & Ola Rune
□ **www.livingdivani.it**

Toop (2000) by Eero Koivisto
□ **www.david.se**

Glo-ball floorlamp (1998),
Jasper Morrison ▫ **www.flos.net**

Luminator floorlamp and uplighter (1954),
Achille & Pier Giacomo Castiglioni ▫ **www.flos.net**

Bestlite reading lamp (1930), Robert Dudley Best
▫ **www.bestandlloyd.co.uk**

Stool Model No. 60 in birch (1932–33),
Alvar Aalto ▫ **www.artek.fi**

Lounge Chair No. 670 & Ottoman No. 671 in black leather (1956),
Charles & Ray Eames ▫ **www.vitra.com**

Sky High
by Simon Allford at
Allford Hall Monaghan Morris
www.ahmm.co.uk

The brief for this modest urban apartment at
the top of a late nineteenth-century, red-brick
mansion block was to open up the spaces and
bring in as much natural light as possible.
In stripping the place back to its shell, the
ceilings were removed to add to the quality of
space by making the rooms taller. Rooflights were
also added. Doors to small roof terraces extend
the space outwards. Luxurious detailing includes
the use of rich walnut wood throughout for all
joinery. The collection of modern classic furniture
and lighting sits comfortably in this elegant
setting.

1 Wall-fixed magazine rack from Paustian
▫ **www.paustian.dk**

2 The credenza was constructed by a local joinery firm
▫ **for furniture designers and makers, see the Directory
of Suppliers on pages 152–55**

3 Élan sofa in black leather by Jasper Morrison, part
of a modular seating system ▫ **www.cappellini.it**

4 Op-la tray table (1998) by Jasper Morrison.
Stainless steel base with ABS plastic tray table top
▫ **www.alessi.com**

5 Cork tiles are much underrated as a floorcovering;
they are natural and warm, and easy to install. Suppliers
are fewer in number than in the 1970s, when cork
enjoyed a period of popularity, but many good flooring
supply companies will have cork tiles somewhere on their
product lists ▫ **for natural floorcoverings, including cork
tiles, see the Directory of Suppliers on pages 152–55**

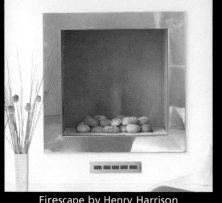

The Matrix
□ **www.verine.co.uk**

Firescape by Henry Harrison
□ **www.platonicfireplaces.co.uk**

Firescheme by Henry Harrison
□ **www.platonicfireplaces.co.uk**

Jolly Mec Caldea
□ **www.jolly-mec.it**

Bathyscafocus by Dominique Imbert
□ **www.focus-creation.com**

Fire Line
□ **www.cvo.co.uk**

The Metro
□ **www.chesneys.co.uk**

Classic 106
□ **www.rais.dk**

Agorafocus ceiling suspended fireplace, Dominique Imbert □ **www.focus-creation.com**

Costanza adjustable floorlamp (1985), Paolo Rizzatto □ **www.luceplan.com**

Oxchair in black leather (1960), Hans J. Wegner □ **www.erik-joergensen.com**

Grown-up time
by Magnus Ståhl Architect

www.staahl.com

The converted attic space of this large family house is a tranquil area where the parents can withdraw to at the end of a long day. The room has been treated as simply as possible with solid oak flooring and white walls and ceiling, which is finished in painted wood planking for a light yet warm effect. Floor-to-ceiling, metal-frame sliding doors lead onto a small terrace. There's also a guest room and shower room up here, with the shower opening directly onto the terrace.

1 The entire space is lined with timber boarding that has then been painted white – the effect is charming and distantly reminiscent of log cabins, ships interiors or even, perhaps, a treehouse □ **for wood cladding, see the Directory of Suppliers on pages 152–55**

2 Punktlampan spot lights in aluminium by Focus Belysning. The lights protrude slightly from the ceiling. Available in four different sizes □ **www.foxdesign.se**

3 Built-in cupboards designed by the architect. The oak doors open out and then slide back into the wall. One cupboard contains a TV, the other a music system □ **www.staahl.com**

4 Coffee table in oak. Similar designs include George (2001) and Solo (1999) by Antonio Citterio □ **www.bebitalia.it**

5 Charles sofa with soft taupe upholstery (1998) by Antonio Citterio □ **www.bebitalia.it**

6 Solid oak parquet flooring □ **for wood flooring, including parquet, see the Directory of Suppliers on pages 152–55**

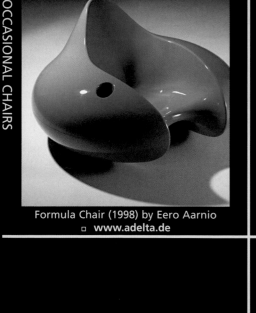

Formula Chair (1998) by Eero Aarnio
□ **www.adelta.de**

Sacco (1968) by Piero Gatti, Cesare Paolini &
Franco Teodoro □ **www.zanotta.it**

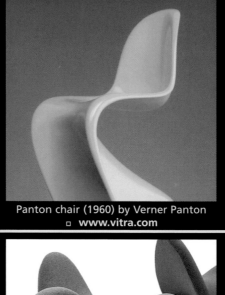

Panton chair (1960) by Verner Panton
□ **www.vitra.com**

Dodo by Mårten Claesson, Eero Koivisto
& Ola Rune □ **www.eandy.com**

Model No. 577, Tongue (1967) by
Pierre Paulin □ **www.artifort.com**

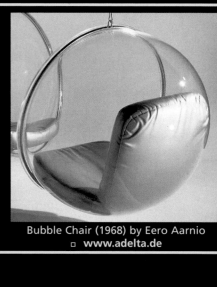

Bubble Chair (1968) by Eero Aarnio
□ **www.adelta.de**

Wiggle (1972) by Frank O. Gehry
□ **www.vitra.com**

Ball Chair (1966) by Eero Aarnio
□ **www.adelta.de**

S-chair (1988) by Tom Dixon
□ **www.cappellini.it**

Canadian Hard Maple kitchen system
□ **www.poggenpohl.de**

Fibreglass chair (1948–50), Charles & Ray Eames,
reissued as Plastic Chair □ **www.vitra.com**

hm26 sofa in brown leather, Fred Scott
□ **www.hitchmylius.co.uk**

Modern classic
by David Bishop at Bluebottle

www.bluebottle.co.uk

In this conversion of a late nineteenth-century brick-built factory, the open-plan layout makes an ideal space for supper and parties with friends. The architect stripped out the space to create an empty shell and then inserted a minimalist interior, which retains the great sense of space. The owner is a fan of post-war design classics and has spent years scouring markets, auction rooms and second-hand stores to find his impressive collection of 1950s, '60s and '70s furniture, lighting, glassware, ceramics and sculpture.

1 An entire wall of built-in cupboards was designed by the architect to hide the services, provide a huge amount of storage space and enable the rest of the open-plan room to remain uncluttered. The cupboards are just 30cm deep and sheer doors without handles reduce their visual impact on the room □ **www.bluebottle.co.uk**

2 This lamp was discovered in a second-hand store. A French design from the 1960s, it's called Sputnik □ **for vintage furniture and home accessories, see the Directory of Suppliers on pages 152–55**

3 Wooden abstract sculpture by British artist Brian Willsher
□ **www.geocities.com/brianwillsher**

4 The bar stools are a second-hand find; they have been reupholstered in a cream fabric. The style is similar to the Polo bar stool by Robin Day, based on his classic Polo chair (1973) □ **www.loftonline.net**

5 Oversized table made from 4-metre long scaffolding boards, which were sanded and then stained a dark teak colour to match the floor
□ **for architectural salvage and recycled timber, see the Directory of Suppliers on pages 152–55**

6 Reclaimed teak floorboards from an old university building, sanded and finished with Danish oil, which seeps into the surface and hardens to leave a matt surface □ **www.liberon.com**

7 Again a second-hand find, the lounge chairs have moulded plywood shells standing on a stem foot. They are similar in shape to armchair Model No. 545, Tulip (1965) by Pierre Paulin □ **www.artifort.com**

8 Woollen shagpile rug completes the 1960s look of this great interior. For the ultimate in softness look out for sheepskin rugs
□ **www.boconcept.com**

Model No. PK61 (1955) by Poul Kjærholm
□ **www.fritzhansen.com**

Model No. E1027, Adjustable Table (1927)
by Eileen Gray □ **www.classicon.com**

Lift-Up by Mårten Claesson, Eero Koivisto
& Ola Rune □ **www.nola.se**

Isokon Nesting Tables (1936) by
Marcel Breuer □ **www.isokonplus.com**

Model No. 780/783 (1966) by
Gianfranco Frattini □ **www.cassina.it**

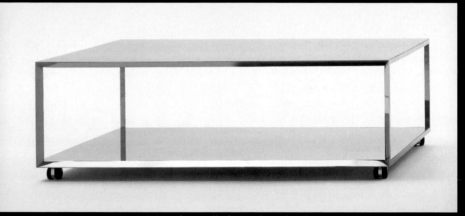

Ministeel Carrello by Carlo Colombo
□ **www.cappellini.it**

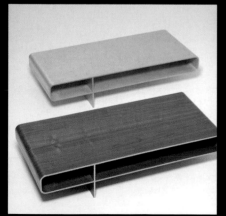

Loop (1996) by Barber Osgerby
□ **www.isokonplus.com**

Kite (2003) by Andreas Weber
□ **www.desalto.it**

Model No. 634, Schroeder 1 (1922–23) by
Gerrit Thomas Rietveld □ **www.cassina.it**

Tolomeo floor lamp in aluminium (1987), Michele de Lucchi & Giancarlo Fassina □ www.artemide.com

Lounge Chair No. 670 & Ottoman No. 671 in black leather (1956), Charles & Ray Eames □ www.vitra.com

Tulip small side table with white marble table top (1956), Eero Saarinen □ www.knollint.com

Rich comfort

by Pablo Uribe

www.studiouribe.com

The refurbishment of this nineteenth-century urban apartment was designed to create a sense of warm modernity. Period details, including the windows with their pretty colour glass panels and the cast-iron fireplace, were saved and restored and then the new finishes carefully installed. Walls are a soft khaki colour and the floor is a rich merbau timber. Into the space a mixture of classic and contemporary furniture has been introduced to give an uncluttered modern yet homely look.

1 Bespoke lighting designed by Peter Nelson for SKK □ www.skk.net

2 Modular metal wall-fixed shelving system □ www.fontanaarte.it

3 Art nouveau-style, cast-iron original fireplace, which has been cleaned up and given a matt black finish □ **for architectural salvage, including fireplaces, see the Directory of Suppliers on pages 152–55**

4 Costanza table lamp (1985) by Paolo Rizzatto. Available as floor, table and pendant lamps, as well as wall lights, with a square natural aluminium stand, which is also available painted black or iron grey. The lamp features a dimmer rod close to the light, which only has to be touched to adjust its brightness through four levels. The silk-screen printed polycarbonate shade is available in a range of colours □ **www.luceplan.com**

5 Apta Collection bench table by Antonio Citterio. Shown in wenge wood on stainless steel frame □ **www.maxalto.it**

6 A vintage find, this much sought-after ebonised credenza is by Florence Knoll from 1961 □ **for vintage furniture, see the Directory of Suppliers on pages 152–55** □ Now part of the Florence Knoll Executive Collection, the credenza is still in production under the brand of Knoll Studio □ **www.knoll.com**

7 Richly coloured, merbau hardwood floor gives a warm tone to the room. This was bought as a prefinished system floor, with a good 4mm depth of veneer protected with six coats of lacquer □ **for wood flooring, see the Directory of Suppliers on pages 152–55**

8 Charles sofa in dark grey upholstery (1998) by Antonio Citterio. Shown with Charles bench in lighter grey fabric □ **www.bebitalia.it**

Lampadina (1972) by Achille Castiglioni
□ **www.flos.net**

Astrobaby (1963) by Edward Craven-Walker
□ **www.mathmos.com**

Miss Sissi (1991) by Philippe Starck
□ **www.flos.net**

Aoy (1975) by Achille Castiglioni
□ **www.flos.net**

Glo-ball (1998) by Jasper Morrison
□ **www.flos.net**

Double Square Light (1998) by
Marcel Wanders □ **www.moooi.com**

Mezzachimera (1966) by Vico Magistretti
□ **www.artemide.com**

Tulip dining table and chair (1956),
Eero Saarinen □ **www.knollint.com**

Panthella table lamp in white acrylic (1970),
Verner Panton □ **www.louis-poulsen.com**

Living It Up
by A-EM Architects

www.a-em.com

This steel, timber and glass structure demonstrates the potential of under-used city rooftops to create contemporary homes. The apartment, with its city-wide views, sits above an undistinguished low-rise, purpose-built block of 1970s flats. Access to the space was created by fitting a stair where there had been a cupboard in the floor below. The highly desirable apartment has floor-to-ceiling walls of glass wrapping round the open-plan living space. Doors slide open for access to the roof terrace. The owners have fitted blinds only to the more enclosed bedrooms and from the living space enjoy the ever-changing cityscape.

1 Glo-ball pendant lamp (1998) by Jasper Morrison. A series of floor, table and pendant lamps, which give a warm, ambient light. The floor and table lamps stand on slender stem with large circular base
□ **www.flos.net**

2 Monkey children's toy (1951) by Kay Bojesen
□ **www.rosendahl.com**

3 Bespoke shelving designed by the architect using easily available brackets to hold glass shelving □ **www.a-em.com**

4 An unusual, bespoke fireplace designed by the architect. Ceiling-suspended fireplaces in contemporary interiors are extremely eyecatching □ **www.a-em.com**

5 A classic glass coffee table is a good choice for such a glassy structure, it is functional and yet doesn't appear to fill up the space. A glass two-tier table can be found in the series designed by Terence Woodgate for SCP □ **www.scp.co.uk** □ or there's the Sanzeno table (1995) by Emaf Progetti □ **www.zanotta.it**

6 Freetime sofa (1999) by Antonio Citterio. Forms part of a versatile seating system. The design comprises a bright chrome, tubular metal frame with upholstered cushions sitting on a choice of white, blue or black belting which gives a distinctive look and is ecologically sound. The system includes sofas and armchairs with double upholstering for the backrest and seat; and corner units with adjustable backrest and with or without relax movement □ **www.bebitalia.it**

Pierre ou Paul (1996) by Ingo Maurer
□ **www.ingo-maurer.com**

Artichoke (1958) by Poul Henningsen
□ **www.louis-poulsen.com**

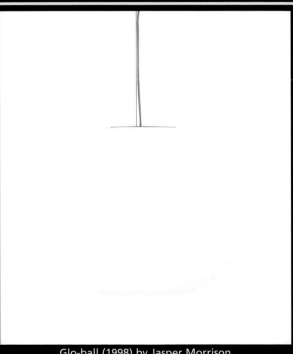

Taraxacum 88 (1988) by Achille Castiglioni
□ **www.flos.net**

Glo-ball (1998) by Jasper Morrison
□ **www.flos.net**

Satellite by Vilhelm Wohlert
□ **www.louis-poulsen.com**

Egg chair (1957) in wicker suspended on a nickel-plated chain, Nanna & Jørgen Ditzel □ **www.bonacinapierantonio.it**

Jack Light floorlamp (1996), Tom Dixon □ **www.eurolounge.co.uk**

Urban eyrie
by Featherstone Associates
www.featherstone-associates.co.uk

This laid back living space, complete with sunken seating area, sits at the very top of an extremely unusual courtyard house. In a restricted urban site, the architect has succeeded in creating an intriguing home which starts at street level with a modest door set in a blank brick wall. Inside, the stairway climbs to one side of an open courtyard. Sleeping and bathing areas occupy the lower parts of the building, and as it climbs more light is drawn into the rooms. At the top, the space explodes open into a large kitchen and dining room with steps up to this living space. A further short flight of stairs leads to a rooftop terrace with spectacular city views.

1 Porcelain pendant lamps hung in profusion were from ProtoUK, a company which no longer exists. For more ideas for pendant fittings visit Tecnolumen □ **www.tecnolumen.de** □ Luceplan □ **www.luceplan.com** □ and Foscarini □ **www.foscarini.com**

2 Brightly coloured, upholstered chairs, bought secondhand in a local street market. Among those making soft sculptural upholstered chairs are Edra □ **www.edra.com** □ Arflex □ **www.arflex.com** □ and ClassiCon □ **www.classicon.com**

3 Sunken seating area. A soft, upholstered seating pit is the perfect place to chill out, light from the window and rooflight is diffused by the muslin curtain □ **for fabrics, see the Directory of Suppliers on pages 152–55**

4 Seating Pad in blue foam by Michael Young □ **www.cappellini.it**

5 Peran Rustik Glamour pebble flooring in white by Perstorp □ **www.peran.com**

6 Timber flooring in elm, along with other joinery in the house, was completed by Dominic Ash □ **www.dominicash.co.uk**

Prototype (2001) by Bernhard Dessecker &
Ingo Maurer □ **www.ingo-maurer.com**

Floor lamp JL2L (1997) by Juha Leiviskä
□ **www.artek.fi**

Brera F (1992) by Achille Castiglioni
□ **www.flos.net**

Clitunno (1963) by Vico Magistretti
□ **www.artemide.com**

Set Up Shades (1989) by Marcel Wanders
□ **www.moooi.com**

Luminator (1954) by Achille &
Pier Giacomo Castiglioni□ **www.flos.net**

Taccia (1962) by Achille &
Pier Giacomo Castiglioni□ **www.flos.net**

AJ (1957–60) by Arne Jacobsen
□ **www.louis-poulsen.com**

Arco floorlamp with marble base (1962),
Achille & Pier Giacomo Castiglioni □ **www.flos.net**

Costanza adjustable floorlamp (1985),
Paolo Rizzatto □ **www.luceplan.com**

Urban living
by Fiona Mclean at Mclean Quinlan

www.mcleanquinlan.com

The owner of this protected historic townhouse enjoys the contrast of old and new. The eighteenth-century building retains many original details including window shutters and ceiling mouldings, which have been painted white to form a neutral backdrop to the contemporary interior. The muted greys are given an exciting boost by the red bench.

1 Bespoke grey Acero limestone fire surround, in a contemporary style to complement the interior □ **for fires, stoves and fireplaces, see the Directory of Suppliers on pages 152–55**

2 SFS 03 digital television with 75cm flat screen
□ **www.panasonic.com**

3 Slender slatted birch blinds, which have been fitted to filter and soften the powerful afternoon sun in this west-facing room □ **for blinds, see the Directory of Suppliers on pages 152–55**

4 Charles sofa in grey imitation suede (1998) by Antonio Citterio
□ **www.bebitalia.it** □ upholstered in Glove □ **www.kvadrat.dk**

5 Charles bench in red wool (1998) by Antonio Citterio
□ **www.bebitalia.it** □ upholstered in Scarlet □ **www.butefabrics.com**

6 Fra table with white lacquered table top by Roberto Barbieri. The frame is flat steel available in black, graphite or nickeled varnish
□ **www.bebitalia.it**

7 Grey linen and wool mix flatweave rug, which complements the grey of the sofa and anchors the room □ **www.kasthall.se**

8 Solid oak flooring, which has been finished in a subtle matt varnish to provide the room with a warm colour base □ **for wood flooring, see the Directory of Suppliers on pages 152–55**

• the dining table is a key item of furniture – dark wood and antique pieces have a more formal feel than pale wood and contemporary styles

• comfortable dining chairs are a must unless you want guests to leave early – choose a design that combines comfortable seats with a shaped back rest for good support

• for a formal style, use rich, dark colours; for informality choose lighter, fresher colours

• storage space close to the table is extremely useful, a dresser or sideboard is ideal for serving bowls, place mats, glasses, candles, linen and even cutlery and crockery

• dimmer controls on the lighting make it easy to switch from bright upbeat moods, to a quieter, more restful atmosphere

• candles may be a cliché, but they do provide a calming, flattering and romantic light

In most homes the dining room is an endangered space, separate dining rooms are often converted into home offices or knocked through into the living room. Despite our increasingly informal attitude to meal times, most homes retain a dining table which becomes the focus for entertaining and there remain plenty of occasions of the space – a polished, dark wood, antique piece of furniture has a more formal feel to it than a light oak refectory table. Chairs need to be chosen carefully, too. To save space, stacking and folding chairs are a good idea, but comfort should always be a priority, especially if you enjoy people sitting round the table talking for

DINING ROOMS

when sharing food with friends and family is a thoroughly enjoyable way to pass the time. In an open-plan space, the ideal table should complement any existing furnishings. Where space is limited, it may need to be a design that folds up and stows away. In a designated dining room, the choice of table is key to the character hours. Lighting certainly helps to set the mood – bright light levels are fine for children's tea parties, but can be uncomfortable for grown-up suppers, so dimmer switches are useful. A pendant lamp over the table helps to make the plates and glasses sparkle, and candles always cast a restful, flattering and romantic light.

Double Decker (2001) by Marcel Wanders
□ **www.moooi.com**

Strata by Edward Carpenter & Rushton Bros
□ **www.timeframe.info**

Table 81B (1933–35) by Alvar Aalto
□ **www.artek.fi**

Arc by Mårten Claesson, Eero Koivisto & Ola Rune
□ **www.asplund.org**

Dining Table 746 (1941) by Jens Risom
□ **www.knoll.com**

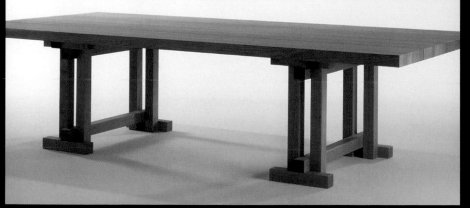

Level Table by Peter Emrys-Roberts
□ **www.driade.com**

Model No. 2650, Leonardo (1950) by Achille Castiglioni
□ **www.zanotta.it**

Lem barstool in white leather (2000),
Shin & Tomoko Azumi □ www.lapalma.it

Rondo chair in white laminate,
Erik Jørgensen □ www.danerka.dk

Minimal Dining Table in walnut, De La Espada
□ www.delaespada.com

Polished finish
by Denton Corker Marshall Architects

www.dcm-group.com

Glass, cedar, zinc and concrete have been combined to create this contemporary home and studio with roof garden on a small urban plot, previously occupied by old stables, and overlooking a park. Designed for an Australian photographer and his art director wife in London, the living space floats above the entire ground-floor studio. At its heart is a spacious dining, cooking and living area where the architect has played with blurring the boundaries between inside and out by building in huge sliding doors, which open up one corner entirely to make the room feel like an open terrace.

1 Bespoke kitchen system designed by the architect. The sheer, white-lacquered doors are push release. The island unit features an inset panel of walnut veneer, which links to the walnut dining table □ **www.dcm-group.com**

2 Raised up on a concrete plinth to maximise its effect as a focal point of the space, this bespoke hearth houses a contemporary gas fire. The special heat-tolerant stones are made to resemble pebbles □ **www.realflame.co.uk**

3 Gorki collection sofa (2002) in purple fabric upholstery by Rodolfo Dordoni. Collection includes a coordinating bench. Available in fabric upholstery or leather □ **www.minotti.it**

4 An antique find, the stainless-steel, glass and wood coffee table by Merrow Associates is probably from the 1970s □ **for vintage furniture, see the Directory of Suppliers on pages 152–55**

5 Geometric lamp with decorative shade from Maisonette, which complements the vintage coffee table □ **www.maisonette.uk.com**

6 The surface of the structural concrete floor has been painstakingly ground to produce this amazing polished finish □ **for concrete flooring, see the Directory of Suppliers on pages 152–55**

Cherner Chair (1958) by Paul Goldman
□ **www.chernerchair.com**

Butterfly Chair (1958) by Lucian R. Ercolani
□ **www.ercol.com**

Model No. 699, Superleggera by Gio Ponti □ **www.cassina.it**

LCM (1945) by Charles & Ray Eames
□ **www.vitra.com**

DCM (1945) by Charles & Ray Eames
□ **www.vitra.com**

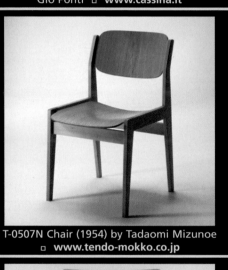

T-0507N Chair (1954) by Tadaomi Mizunoe
□ **www.tendo-mokko.co.jp**

Pop by Eero Koivisto
□ **www.offecct.se**

Model No. 214 (1859) by Michael Thonet
□ **www.thonet.de**

S-7260B Chair (1955) by Charlotte Perriand
□ **www.tendo-mokko.co.jp**

Bend by Mårten Claesson
□ **www.swedese.se**

Dining feast
by Claesson Koivisto Rune
www.claesson-koivisto-rune.se

In a dramatic bid to open up this large apartment, walls came down and transformed the place from seven rooms to just three main free-flowing spaces for sitting, cooking and eating and sleeping. This handsome home, once the Soviet ambassador's residence in Stockholm, is on the third floor of a 1920s city-centre block. It has windows on three sides and is blessed with generous sunlight. The preparatory work entailed removing walls and stripping out some of the old interior, but the architects left in place much of the original plaster mouldings and decorative architraving 'so that the new additions could be seen in clear contrast with the backdrop of the old.' Walls were painted white and, where damaged, the oak flooring was restored and then given a white-limed finish. In such large spaces, rugs can be used effectively to define different areas.

1 Bespoke dining table designed by the architects, Mårten Claesson, Eero Koivisto and Ola Rune. This monumental table was made from a single African walnut tree trunk. Measuring 4.5m in length, it had to be craned into the third-floor apartment through a window □ **www.claesson-koivisto-rune.se**

2 Smith, a flat bowl or fruit plate, by Eero Koivisto □ **www.david.se**

3 Line rug in natural and brown by Ritva Puotila. This is one of a basic collection of 56 designs created out of the harmonious combinations of six patterns and 11 colour alternatives. Unusually, the rug is made using 86 percent woven paper yarn and 14 percent cotton □ **www.woodnotes.fi**

4 Original oak parquet flooring □ **for wood flooring, including parquet, see the Directory of Suppliers on pages 152–55** □ The parquet flooring has been cleaned, restored and then finished with a white stain □ **www.triptrap.com**

5 Lines rug by Alfredo Häberli. An intriguing carpet in 100 percent New Zealand wool. The textured finish is reminiscent of a ploughed field or rock worn by rivulets of water □ **www.asplund.org**

6 Metro sofa (1999) by Piero Lissoni. Upholstered in grey-blue fabric □ **www.livingdivani.it**

Bolla floor lamp (1999), Michael Sodeau
□ **www.gervasoni1882.com**

Y-chair (1950), also know as the Wishbone chair, Hans J. Wegner □ **www.carlhansen.com**

Model No. 2532, Marcuso (1969) by Marco Zanuso
□ **www.zanotta.it**

Model No. CH008 (1954) by Hans J. Wegner
□ **www.carlhansen.com**

City by Mårten Claesson, Eero Koivisto & Ola Rune
□ **www.irenuffici.com**

Model No. 322, D.S.1 (1918) by Charles Rennie Mackintosh
□ **www.cassina.it**

Model No. P970, Plano by Pelikan Design
□ **www.fritzhansen.com**

Model No. 1312, Dining Table (1966) by Warren Platner
□ **www.knollint.com**

S chair (1988) with woven rush seat,
Tom Dixon □ **www.cappellini.it**

LIM dining table with frosted safety glass table top,
Bruno Fattorini/Studio MDF □ **www.mdfitalia.it**

The Classic radiator, Bisque
□ **www.bisque.co.uk**

JIM dining chairs (1999) with red upholstery,
Gijs Papavoine □ **www.montis.nl**

Monumental scale
by David Mikhail Architects

www.davidmikhail.com

This airy dining and kitchen area was created during
the refurbishment and extension of a listed townhouse.
The architect's clever space engineering involved dropping
the level of the floor into what had been a dark basement
to produce an extremely tall room with direct access to
the garden. To emphasise the monumental feel of the
space, a huge, 4m-tall sliding cedar door now leads to
the outside terrace. Additional top light enters the kitchen
through a silicon-jointed glass box, which has been added
to the roof.

1 Bespoke geometric, built-in wall cupboard system designed by
the architect □ **www.davidmikhail.com**

2 Filo pendant lamp (1994) by Peter Christian. The polycarbonate
shade, shown here in orange, is available in a range of colours
□ **www.aktiva.co.uk**

3 Aluminium pendant lamp. Similar pendant lamps are available from
Ikea □ **www.ikea.com**

4 Architectural glass roof with silicon joints □ **for architectural glass,
see the Directory of Suppliers on pages 152–55**

5 Kitchen units designed by the architect □ **www.davidmikhail.com**
□ Made by adapting a basic Ikea system, then finished in white
and grey □ **www.ikea.com**

6 Custom-made stainless-steel worktop and splashback
□ **for kitchen furniture, see the Directory of Suppliers on pages 152–55**

7 D line range by Knud Holscher. This range of handles first
appeared in the 1970s, but continues to be developed. Available in
satin stainless steel □ **www.dline.com**

8 Solid ash floor planks with a 2mm v-joint specified by the architect,
which gives the floor subtle visual interest □ **for wood flooring, see
the Directory of Suppliers on pages 152–55**

9 Oversized, 4m-tall sliding door to the garden designed by the
architect □ **www.davidmikhail.com** □ Constructed in cedar.
Top hung using sliding gear by Geze □ **www.geze.de**

Cornflake by Mårten Claesson, Eero Koivisto
& Ola Rune □ **www.offecct.se**

Polo Chair (1973) by Robin Day
□ **www.loftonline.net**

Model No. PK9, Tulip Chair (1960) by
Poul Kjærholm □ **www.fritzhansen.com**

Doppio by Eero Koivisto
□ **www.offecct.se**

Hudson (2000) by Philippe Starck
□ **www.emeco.net**

Model No. 3107, Series 7 (1955) by
Arne Jacobsen □ **www.fritzhansen.com**

Afternoon (2001) by Eero Koivisto
□ **www.skandiform.se**

T-3047M Ply Chair (1960) by Saburo Inui
□ **www.tendo-mokko.co.jp**

Model No. 1296, Side Chair (1950–52) by
Harry Bertoia □ **www.knollint.com**

Model No. VM101 VicoDuo (1997) by
Vico Magistretti □ **www.fritzhansen.com**

Tulip pedestal dining table with polished white marble table top (1956), Eero Saarinen □ **www.knollint.com**

Series 7 chairs (1955) with white laminate seats, Arne Jacobsen □ **www.fritzhansen.com**

Bombo barstools (1997) with white ABS plastic seats, Stefano Giovannoni □ **www.magisdesign.com**

White Penthouse

by John Crummay & Robin Rout

www.johncrummay.com □ www.robinrout.com

The designers of this apartment bought the rights to build on the roof of a converted nineteenth-century warehouse apartment. They then constructed a steel and glass rectangular box with a continuous band of horizontal windows, which provides a 360-degree view of the cityscape. The pristine white interior was created to provide an area of calm to contrast with the busy city outside.

1 Lighting throughout is mostly 30mm ceiling-recessed low-voltage halogen downlighters from the Concord range of Sylvania □ **www.syvlania-lighting.com** □ The system is computer controlled to provide a range of mood settings □ **www.lutron.com**

2 Radar armchairs and ottomans in white fabric upholstery by James Irvine □ **www.bebitalia.it**

3 High-backed oak chairs designed by Robert Williams from Pearl Dot □ **email: enq@pearldot.com**

4 Lunar sofa in white fabric upholstery by James Irvine □ **www.bebitalia.it**

5 To complement the industrial aesthetic of the Bulthaup kitchen □ **www.bulthaup.com** □ a metalworking firm was commissioned to wrap the chunky breakfast bar in stainless steel □ **for kitchen furniture, see the Directory of Suppliers on pages 152–55**

6 The high-gloss white flooring looks like timber planks but is, in fact, custom-made using fire-retardant and moisture-resistant MDF with bevelled edges. The tough glossy white coating was spray finished for a smooth sheen using specialist floor paint from the International range □ **www.akzonobel.com**

Model No. 451, La Basilica (1977) by Mario Bellini
□ **www.cassina.it**

Table Y805A (1946–47) by Alvar Aalto
□ **www.artek.fi**

Model No. CH006 (1982) by Hans J. Wegner
□ **www.carlhansen.com**

Bend by Mårten Claesson, Eero Koivisto & Ola Rune
□ **www.swedese.se**

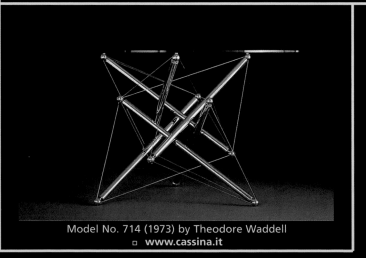

Model No. 714 (1973) by Theodore Waddell
□ **www.cassina.it**

Space engineers
by Plastik Architects
www.plastik-architects.net

One of the architect's most impressive skills is space engineering, which was certainly put to good use in this modest-size Victorian terrace house that was refurbished and opened up for its current owners. Because the budget for the refurbishment works was fairly restrained, the remodelling had to be subtle yet effective. The ground floor had comprised two small rooms, so to open them up and connect them visually a former window has been opened to the ground to mirror the doorway in the separating wall. The dining space now benefits from extra natural lighting entering through the glassy kitchen extension beyond. Floor-to-ceiling shelves provide valuable storage for the owner's impressive book collection. The choice of a glass-topped table ensures that lightflow and views are uninterrupted through the space, which helps to make it feel larger, and the circular shape is a well-chosen space-efficient design. White chairs helps to keep the space bright and airy.

1 Ceiling-recessed lights are often chosen for small spaces in place of pendant lights because they provide good quality, sparkling light and don't distract the eye □ **for lighting, see the Directory of Suppliers on pages 152–55**

2 Floor-to-ceiling shelving is the most space-efficient type and provides room for displaying objects together with storing books. Designed by the architect and made on site by the building contractor. By painting the shelves white, the same colour as the wall, they recede visually □ **www.plastik-architects.net**

3 The sheer finish of the oak floor also helps to make the space look and feel streamlined □ **for wood flooring, see the Directory of Suppliers on pages 152–55**

4 A cowhide rug sourced by the client adds extra texture and pattern to the room □ **for carpets and rugs, see the Directory of Suppliers on pages 152–55**

Vintage dining table, for similar see La Rotonda (1976), Mario Bellini □ **www.cassina.it**

Rondo chair in white laminated plywood, Erik Jørgensen □ **www.danerka.dk**

Model No. 150, Tulip Chair (1956) by
Eero Saarinen ▫ **www.knollint.com**

Model No. 100, Follia (1934) by
Giuseppe Terragni ▫ **www.zanotta.it**

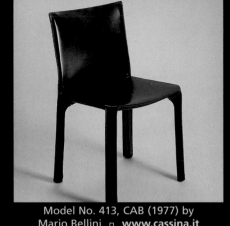

Model No. 413, CAB (1977) by
Mario Bellini ▫ **www.cassina.it**

Model No. S32 (1929–30) by
Marcel Breuer ▫ **www.thonet.de**

Model No. S664 by Eddie Harlis
▫ **www.thonet.de**

Classica (1996) by Piero Lissoni
▫ **www.cappellini.it**

Model No. 3101, Ant Chair (1952) by
Arne Jacobsen ▫ **www.fritzhansen.com**

Model No. 2015, Viola (1997) by
Tamar Ben David ▫ **www.zanotta.it**

Model No. 2090, Tonietta (1985) by
Enzo Mari ▫ **www.zanotta.it**

Fucsia 3 pendant lamp (1996),
Achille Castiglioni □ **www.flos.net**

DCM (Dining Chair Metal) in black plywood (1945),
Charles & Ray Eames □ **www.vitra.com**

Bespoke dining

by Featherstone Associates & Dominic Ash

www.featherstone-associates.co.uk □

www.dominicash.co.uk

Forming part of a converted office building, this apartment was bought by the owners during the conversion works. Their early purchase enabled them to organise the spaces exactly as they wanted for their young family. With the help of the architect, they achieved three bedrooms, instead of the two planned by the developer, and oriented the living space to the south west in order to overlook the local park. They also gained planning permission to build in additional windows, which flood the interior with natural sunlight. Much of the furniture, using a variety of different woods, has been designed and made by one of the owners, furniture maker Dominic Ash.

1 Wall of kitchen units by Dominic Ash. Built using beech veneer with glossy spray-painted white doors. The doors incorporate a neat indented finger-pull detail to avoid the use of handles, which would spoil the sheer finish. The white of the units helps them to meld into the white of the wall □ **for furniture designers and makers, see the Directory of Suppliers on pages 152–55**

2 Mosaic mirror tiles, readily available in most home stores, add jolly sparkle □ **for tiles, see the Directory of Suppliers on pages 152–55**

3 American black walnut was selected as the material for the island unit, also by Dominic Ash. It was chosen for its warmth and as a contrast to the white of the cupboards. The unit houses the oven, hob, a set of drawers and a waste bin. To bring out the grain and for a lustrous finish, the wood is finished with a natural oil, as is the table and the bench unit □ **for furniture designers and makers, see the Directory of Suppliers on pages 152–55**

4 Dining table designed by Dominic Ash and made in rich-coloured wenge wood □ **for furniture designers and makers, see the Directory of Suppliers on pages 152–55**

5 The bench, designed and made by Dominic Ash, is in American black walnut and provides storage for CDs, DVDs and videos □ **for furniture designers and makers, see the Directory of Suppliers on pages 152–55**

6 The ash floor is laid over under-floor heating, it is given an oiled finish □ **for wood flooring, see the Directory of Suppliers on pages 152–55**

Unit by Mårten Claesson, Eero Koivisto & Ola Rune
□ **www.asplund.org**

Model No. 750, Florence (1999) by Alfredo Häberli
□ **www.zanotta.it**

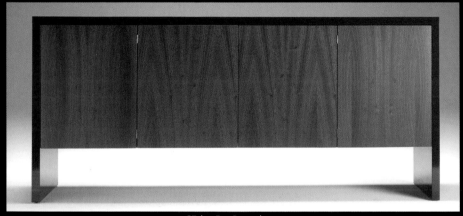

C5 by Bo Steenberg
□ **www.opus1living.com**

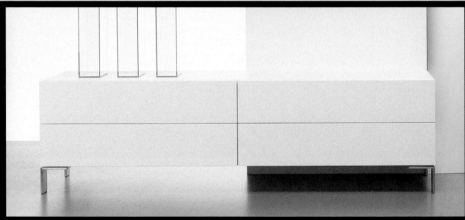

Segno by Carlo Colombo
□ **www.cappellini.it**

Wing (1999) by Michael Sodeau
□ **www.isokonplus.com**

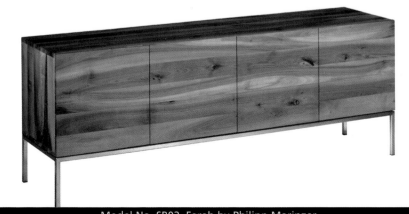

Model No. SB02, Farah by Philipp Marinzer
□ **www.e15.com**

PH 3/2 table lamps (1926),
Poul Henningsen □ **www.louis-poulsen.com**

Antique sideboard clad in stainless steel,
Tony Heine □ **www.heinedesign.com**

Barcelona chair (1929) in black leather,
Ludwig Mies van der Rohe □ **www.knoll.com**

Antique Chic
by Heine Design

www.heinedesign.com

This former bakery in the heart of Copenhagen was gutted, walls were torn down and the whole space reinvented as an open-plan apartment by its owner, furniture designer Tony Heine. The interior is used to show off some of Heine's more unusual creations, such as the antique-and-modern dining table.

1 Triax pendant lamp □ **www.herstal.dk**

2 KV6 two-handled mixer tap (1969) by Arne Jacobsen □ **www.vola.com**

3 Custom-made kitchen units designed by the owner. The small white island unit has a stainless steel top □ **www.heinedesign.com**

4 A metal shelving unit on wheels from the industrial ranges designed for kitchens, laboratories, factories, etc. by shelving and storage expert Metro □ **www.metro.com**

5 The humidor in cherry wood and antique cut-glass decanters are all antique-shop finds □ **for vintage furniture and home accessories, see the Directory of Suppliers on pages 152–55**

6 These sensually curved legs originally belonged to an antique oak table. Because the table top was split and impossible to repair, Heine kept just the legs and incorporated them into a new steel-framed table with a 5mm-glass top □ **www.heinedesign.com**

7 The provenance of these black and aluminium chairs is uncertain, however, they bear a strong resemblance to some classic designs that remain in production, including Polo Chair (1977) by Robin Day □ **www.loftonline.net** □ and Box Chair (1975–6) by Enzo Mari □ **www.driade.com**

8 The original solid oak floor has been finished with an opaque white varnish □ **for wood flooring, see the Directory of Suppliers on pages 152–55**

9 Brown leather covered ottoman with stainless steel legs by Heine Design □ **www.heinedesign.com**

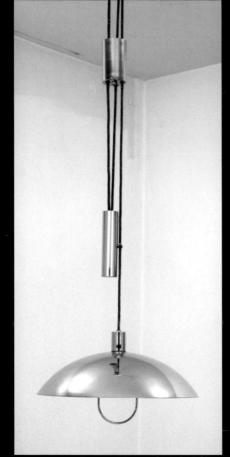

Fucsia 8 (1996) by Achille Castiglioni
□ **www.flos.net**

HMB 25 (1925) by Marianne Brandt &
Hans Przyrembel □ **www.tecnolumen.com**

Zettel'z (1997) by Ingo Maurer
□ **www.ingo-maurer.com**

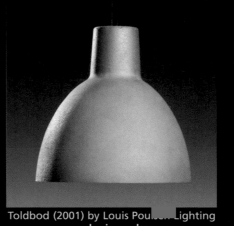

Cup 110S (2003) by Robert Pamio
□ **www.iguzzini.com**

Square Boon (2002) by Piet Boon
□ **www.moooi.com**

Toldbod (2001) by Louis Poulsen Lighting
□ **www.louis-poulsen.com**

Romeo Moon S2 (1996) by Philippe Starck
□ **www.flos.net**

Danish design pendant lamp, for similar see
□ www.louis-poulsen.com or www.flos.net

Alvar Aalto Collection vase (1936),
Alvar Aalto □ www.iittala.com

Room to breathe
by Wahlström and Steijner Architects
www.wahlstrom-steijner.se

The architect's concept for this house was to combine light, space and ecology. Close to the shore, the contemporary-style timber house has been designed to maximise the great sea views, and includes a sundeck on the roof for a panoramic view of the Gothenburg Archipelago, Sweden. Inside, the ground floor is a private zone with bedrooms, bathroom and laundry, while upstairs is this large open living space with sea views. The house incorporates numerous ecological features including healthy insulation materials and low-odour paint.

1 Piu Avantgarde, a circular stove finished in stainless steel and with a 180 degree glass firedoor □ **www.spartherm.com**

2 Basic/Original sofa, designed by Ire Design Group, made by Ire Mobel □ **www.iremobel.se**

3 Ride-on rocking horse, made by the late Arne Karlsson. A similar rocking horse is also part of the range of classics by Playsam □ **www.playsam.com**

4 Blonde wood dining table, bought in Italy. A table with chamfered top and retro-style splayed legs has been designed by Matthew Hilton for SCP. Called Thin, it is made in American walnut with a glass inset top □ **www.scp.co.uk**

5 A wool rug in a neutral stone colour with a pattern of raised circles □ **www.ikea.com**

6 Italian design, metal frame with woven seat and curved wood back. Bought in Italy. For chairs in a similar style with this curved, embracing backrest, see Roger from Ikea □ **www.ikea.com**

- choose between fitted or unfitted units and furniture; fitted systems generally provide more storage than unfitted

- the character of the space will be created by the kitchen cabinets – sheer laminate doors have a sleek look and are easy to keep clean, wood is softer and more family friendly

- so many appliances are temptingly beautiful; choose only what you need and resist being seduced by gadgetry

- task lighting is essential to safe working – lights should be fitted under wall-fixed cupboards or on the wall so that you avoid working in your own shadow

- the design of kitchen sinks has come a long way in recent years, these are now multi-tasking units with fitted chopping boards, pull-out hose taps, waste disposers and more

- smart handles make a budget kitchen look a million dollars

As we all know, the kitchen is the hub of the home and, in most cases, the hardest working space. When planning a kitchen, the first three considerations are your cooking needs, available space and size of budget. If you cook frequently, it is worth investing in a hard-working space; for those who cook occasionally, the best advice is to of the two. A kitchen's character comes from the units and furniture chosen – the professional style is associated with stainless steel, sheer laminates have an urban look, while natural and painted wood are a softer style. The choice of worktops and flooring underline the choice of cabinet – hardwearing stainless steel is the choice of chefs,

KITCHENS

opt for a modest scheme. Take care when choosing appliances, it is easy to overspend on unnecessary gadgets. The room size has a major influence on a kitchen layout: the smallest spaces can be highly functional when lined with a fitted modular system. In larger rooms there's the option of either a fitted or an unfitted style, or a mixture granite and marble is expensive and chic, laminate is extremely tough and inexpensive, wood is appealing, but usually requires maintenance to keep it looking good. To make the transformation from busy breakfasts to smart suppers, good task lighting combined with flexible and imaginative general lighting is key

Case System 5.0 in stainless steel (2000) by Piero Lissoni
□ **www.boffi.com**

Tecna by Studio Kairos
□ **www.varennapoliform.it**

LT (2002) by Piero Lissoni
□ **www.boffi.com**

Gandhara (2001) by Minotti Cucine
□ **www.minotticucine.it**

Case System 5.0 in white pral (2000) by Piero Lissoni
□ **www.boffi.com**

Tara wall-mounted mixer tap (1991), Sieger Design □ **www.dornbracht.com**

Teak veneer slimline kitchen units with inset stainless splashback □ **www.projectorange.com**

Teak chic
by Project Orange

www.projectorange.com

When the owners took over this nineteenth-century house, it was in a poor state of repair, but had the potential to create an interesting family home. The kitchen was particularly basic with just an old stone sink and one tap. The architect has extended outwards with a frameless glass extension to increase the space by 50 percent and excavated half a metre for a luxurious ceiling height. The new extension has achieved the owners' wish to have more connection with the courtyard, which has been finished with timber decking and can be lit at night.

1 An ingenious space-saving feature of the room is this L-shaped concrete bench seating, which also doubles as part of the structure for the glass extension □ **www.projectorange.com**

2 Teak dining table designed by the architect to match the kitchen units □ **www.projectorange.com**

3 Slabs of Acero blue limestone flooring. To ensure flooring that is properly installed and sealed against staining, always take advice from the supplier □ **for stone flooring, see the Directory of Suppliers on pages 152–55**

4 Stainless steel electrical socket and switch from Wandsworth's Classic Series 2 □ **www.wandsworth-electrical.com**

K10 (2001) by Norbert Wangen
□ **www.norbert-wangen.com**

SC 60 by SieMatic
□ **www.siematic.de**

Grafics (2001–2002) by Leicht Design Studio
□ **www.leicht.de**

Orlando (2001–2002) by Leicht Design Studio
□ **www.leicht.de**

International Style by SieMatic
□ **www.siematic.de**

INXX mixer tap in stainless steel
□ **www.moraarmatur.se**

Beach stainless steel kitchen sink
□ **www.franke.com**

White laminate kitchen units with concealed
handles □ **www.rbarchitecture.com**

Ice white
by Rahel Belatchew Lerdell
www.rbarchitecture.com

This serene galley-style kitchen sits on the first floor of a contemporary-style, timber house that has been cleverly built on a tricky, north-facing hillside site. Along with the difficulties of the plot, the architect owner and designer of the house also had to work within local regulations that restricted the size and height of the building. From the start, every effort was made to turn these constrictions into an advantage. Bedrooms are placed on the ground floor whilst the living room and kitchen are above for optimum light. The horizontal band of windows is designed for enjoying the views and, at the same time, maintains privacy. Echoing the band of windows, a long internal bar counter opening sits between the kitchen and dining areas. Since it is part of the main living area, the architect wanted to integrate the kitchen into the space, so most of the appliances are contained in cupboards. Even the means of opening the cupboards is concealed, there are 'handles' carved into the edge of the doors, so they operate without catches or magnets. The only item which couldn't be hidden was the Gaggenau oven.

1 A big trough of light has been built into the ceiling while additional task lighting for the counter top is provided by small fixtures underneath the upper cupboards □ **www.rbarchitecture.com**

2 A neat and unusual feature is the sound-system speakers which have been fitted into the ceiling. For a range of speakers and a custom installation service see BW Speakers □ **www.bwspeakers.com**

3 Swanstone white counter top. An extremely durable composite material suitable for kitchens and bathrooms, available in a huge range of colours and textures □ **www.swanstone.com**

4 Induction hob by Bosch □ **www.bosch.com**

5 Pine boards stained very dark brown with a water-based stain. For ecologically sound wood stain products see Minwax □ **www.minwax.com** □ or Behr □ **www.behr.com**

Extending Table (2004) by Matthew Hilton
□ **www.scp.co.uk**

AVL Shaker Table (1999) by Joep van Lieshout
□ www.moooi.com

Model No. CH318 (1960) by Hans J. Wegner
□ **www.carlhansen.com**

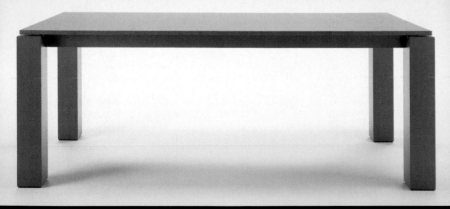

Model No. e6, Dolmen Table by Carlo Colombo
□ **www.poliform.it**

Thin (2001) by Matthew Hilton
□ **www.scp.co.uk**

Concrete and resin mix slab table top on breeze block supports
□ www.icebergarchitecturestudio.com

Ponza dining chair with dark wood finish,
Henri Becq □ www.modenature.com

Rough, polished and painted
by Etienne van den Berg

www.icebergarchitecturestudio.com

The industrial aesthetic of this loft conversion has been continued in the kitchen where concrete – rough, polished and painted – is the predominant material. Vestiges of the original structure, including the cast iron columns and vaulted ceiling, are celebrated by being left exposed. Into this rugged interior has been fitted a refined kitchen, units are given sheet-zinc doors and the counter tops and dining table are constructed in concrete blended with resin for a water- and stainproof finish.

1 To tie in with the front of the cupboard doors, the shelves are also made from zinc □ **for metal and metal workers, see the Directory of Suppliers on pages 152–55**

2 Bespoke kitchen island unit, worktop and dining table designed by the architect □ **www.icebergarchitecturestudio.com** □ All made using concrete that has been blended with resin for a water- and stainproof finish. The material was mixed and poured on site, then smoothed with a trowel. Once dry, the material was given extra protection with a wax finish □ **for concrete worktops, see the Directory of Suppliers on pages 152–55**

3 All appliances in this kitchen, including the dishwasher and refrigerator, are from Smeg □ **www.smeg.it**

4 Walls painted with wipe-clean, matt-finish blackboard paint. Available from the International range □ **www.akzonobel.com**

5 Polished concrete floor slabs □ **for concrete flooring, see the Directory of Suppliers on pages 152–55**

Chair 69 (1933–35) by Alvar Aalto
□ **www.artek.fi**

ERO/S (2001) by Philippe Starck
□ **www.kartell.it**

AVL Shaker Chair (1999) by
Joep van Lieshout □ **www.moooi.com**

DC Chair by Tadhg & Simon O'Driscoll
□ **www.oddesign.com**

Trindad (1993) by Nanna Ditzel
□ **www.fredericia.com**

Model No. e11, Carmel Chair by
Roberto Lazzeroni □ **www.poliform.it**

Model No. 1006, Navy Chair (1940s) by
Emeco □ **www.emeco.net**

Oyster Chair (1998) by Nigel Coates
□ **www.lloydloom.com**

Foto pendant lamp in matt brushed aluminium
□ www.ikea.com

Rotaflow kitchen mixer tap with silk steel finish from the Classic Studio Range □ www.franke.com

Compact Range CPX 652-E stainless steel kitchen sink with silk steel finish from the Classic Studio Range □ www.franke.com

Fibreglass Chair (1948–50), Charles & Ray Eames, now reissued as Plastic Chair □ www.vitra.com

Extreme scheme
by Nick McMahon

email: mail@nickmcmahon.co.uk

The highly unusual and extreme lime green and egg-yolk yellow colour scheme for this kitchen happened entirely by mistake – a mix-up with the contractor. However, the owners have grown to like it, so it has been allowed to remain. The apartment is in a converted meat-processing factory, where the thick concrete walls and floors provided a sturdy shell and the perfect insulation for a residential conversion. The kitchen is formed from a horseshoe-shaped arrangement of units with dining area beyond. This is separated from the living area with a wall of glass bricks.

1 Black mosaic tiles are used as a splashback and given extra interest by the use of white grout □ **for tiles, see the Directory of Suppliers on pages 152–55**

2 Bespoke table with metal trestle-style legs, which features an unusual glass top called Lenscore – a sheet glass sandwich with an aluminium honeycomb centre. It is a material which has been developed by the architect and is extremely strong for its light weight □ **email: mail@nickmcmahon.co.uk**

3 The horseshoe-shaped kitchen is based on a regular 600mm module, but has been custom designed by the architect. It is highly space-efficient, as one wall of units forms a room divider between kitchen and dining areas □ **email: mail@nickmcmahon.co.uk**

4 Beech worktop made from strips of wood. This type of worktop looks great but requires maintenance and care to keep it that way, it doesn't survive well in very damp conditions □ **for wood, including worktops, see the Directory of Suppliers on pages 152–55**

5 The floor is finished in an intriguing end-grain ash, often to be found in industrial flooring, where small tiles of the material are supplied and laid in sheets, like fine parquet □ **for wood flooring, including parquet, see the Directory of Suppliers on pages 152–55** □ The floor is then treated with three coats of matt waterbased sealant □ **www.bona.com**

6 Painting entitled 'Mrs Ballentine and her father with her record salmon' (1992) by Andy Carter

Q Stak (1953) by Robin Day
□ **www.loftonline.net**

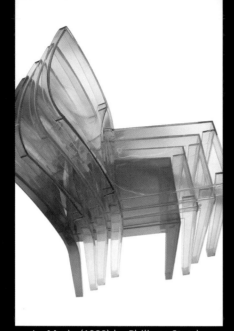

La Marie (1999) by Philippe Starck
□ **www.kartell.it**

Model No. 4867, Universale (1965–67) by Joe Colombo
□ **www.kartell.it**

Stacking Chair (1957) by Lucian R. Ercolani
□ **www.ercol.com**

Tate Contract (2000) by Jasper Morrison
□ **www.cappellini.it**

Model No. KS110, Runner (1997) by Kasper Salto
□ **www.fritzhansen.com**

Byrne (1999) by Eero Koivisto
□ **www.david.se**

1

2

3

Attityd kitchen system, Mikael Warnhammar, adapted by the architect ▫ **www.ikea.com**

La Marie chair in crystal (1999), Philippe Starck ▫ **www.kartell.it**

4

5

See through
by Tonkin Liu

www.tonkinliu.co.uk

In this conversion of a riverside warehouse, at the lower levels of the building light was at a premium. To maximise the sense of light, the architect designed a room which is startlingly transparent. Dining chairs are entirely see through, whilst the kitchen is almost a mirage. Clever lighting design gives the effect of more natural daylight than is the reality. The use of white and grey in the colour scheme helps to reflect light around the space, a device often used in Scandinavian countries where winter sunlight is in short supply. Accessories in cherry red draw the eye around the room.

1 Bespoke lighting designed by the architect ▫ **www.tonkinliu.co.uk** ▫ Above the sink, a long white strip of MDF acts as a baffle for the pair of wall-fixed fluorescent tubes, which sit behind and provide a soft glow ▫ **www.encapsulite.com**

2 The small window has been made to appear much larger and brighter by setting fluorescent strips in the window recesses. A blind pulled down in front of the artificial light makes it appear to be very sunny outside ▫ **www.encapsulite.com**

3 Corian countertop. An extremely tough and almost indestructible product blending natural materials with pure acrylic polymer. It has a silky and luxurious texture ▫ **www.corian.com**

4 Simple white table with a tough white lacquer finish. For a classic white table, see the Maui table (1996) by Vico Magistretti ▫ **www.kartell.it**

5 Standard pine floorboards painted with a pale grey floor paint ▫ **for paint, including floor paint, see the Directory of Suppliers on pages 152–55**

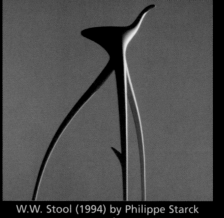

W.W. Stool (1994) by Philippe Starck
□ **www.vitra.com**

Polo (1973) by Robin Day
□ **www.loftonline.net**

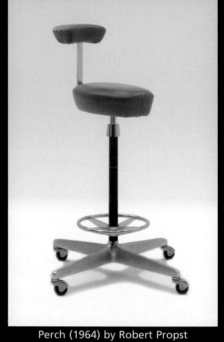

Perch (1964) by Robert Propst
□ **www.hermanmiller.com**

Kong Barstool (2003) by Philippe Starck
□ **www.emeco.net**

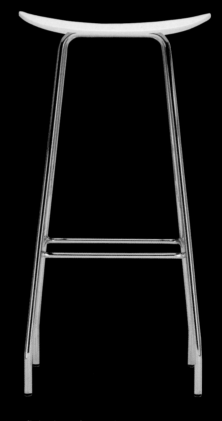

Bombo (1997) by Stefano Giovannoni
□ **www.magisdesign.com**

Grand by Börje Johanson
□ **www.johansondesign.se**

Cornflake by Mårten Claesson, Eero Koivisto
& Ola Rune □ **www.offecct.se**

Model No. 200, Sella (1957) by Achille &
Pier Giacomo Castiglioni □ **www.zanotta.it**

Order of the day
by KSR Architects

www.ksra.co.uk

Generations of piecemeal extensions, which had gradually crept further and further into the garden, were demolished to make way for this contemporary structure. Where once there was a jumble of add-ons now stands one beautifully finished space across the entire width of the house, providing the family with room for a kitchen, dining area and soft seating, all looking over the large garden. The threshold is marked by three huge sliding glass panels, which span the 6m opening that leads onto a decked terrace.

1 Generous natural sunlight falls into the kitchen through this large, custom-designed ceiling rooflight □ **www.ksra.co.uk**

2 Nexus 111 wall-mounted spotlights in matt white □ **www.lightcorporation.com**

3 Ceiling-recessed speakers □ **www.bwspeakers.com**

4 Aluminium sliding doors, consisting of three panels each 2m wide □ **for architectural glass, see the Directory of Suppliers on pages 152–55**

5 Oversized 400 x 400mm tiles in bianco satin white make a refreshing change from their smaller cousins □ **for tiles, see the Directory of Suppliers on pages 152–55**

6 Black Zimbabwean granite worktop □ **for stone worktops, see the Directory of Suppliers on pages 152–55** □ Stone like this should be given a protective seal to prevent staining, so ask your supplier for advice. Many stone specialists suggest using Lithofin products, which include sealants and cleaners □ **www.lithofin.de**

7 Bespoke kitchen, including island with solid oak worktop □ **for kitchen furniture, see the Directory of Suppliers on pages 152–55**

8 Eucalyptus decking □ **for wooden decking, see the Directory of Suppliers on pages 152–55**

9 Aluminium trench heating □ **www.hcp-unilock.co.uk**

10 Solid oak floorboards □ **for wood flooring, see the Directory of Suppliers on pages 152–55**

Lyra barstool with beech seat (1994), Design Group Italia □ www.magisdesign.com

Condor 60 by Villeroy & Boch
□ **www.villeroy-boch.com**

Model No. DB116R by Smeg
□ **www.smeg.it**

Anice by Antonia Astori
□ **www.driade.com**

Cisterna by Villeroy & Boch
□ **www.villeroy-boch.com**

Luna by Villeroy & Boch
□ **www.villeroy-boch.com**

Urban order
by Consarc Architects
with Bluestone Kitchens
www.consarc.co.uk ◻
www.bluestonekitchens.co.uk

A streamlined kitchen in an open-plan living space. This kitchen is designed in a galley style with a single run of units and appliances: it is compact and efficient for city living. The white units looks particularly handsome with the stainless steel appliances and accessories. The entire kitchen is set deep in the apartment close to the dining area, leaving the naturally lit part of the home for the main living space.

1 Under-unit lighting by Delta Light
◻ **www.deltalight.com**

2 Cox basin mixer tap ◻ **www.paini.com**

3 All the appliances, including the built-in oven, extractor and stainless steel fridge-freezer, are by Zanussi
◻ **www.zanussi.com**

Carisma circular stainless steel sink and drainer ◻ **www.carron.com**

Kuji White Range modular kitchen system
◻ **www.bluestonekitchens.co.uk**

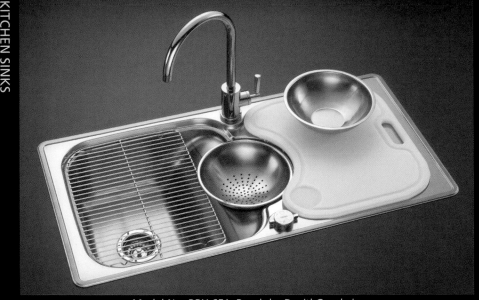

Model No. BBX 651, Beach by David Goodwin
□ **www.franke.com**

Alien series, Model No. BX25.5SS by Baumatic
□ **www.baumatic.com**

Model No. MTG 651, Mythos by F.A. Porsche
□ **www.franke.com**

Model No. CPX 651, Compact (1979) by Franke
□ **www.franke.com**

Triano by Villeroy & Boch
□ **www.villeroy-boch.com**

KV1 by Arne Jacobsen
□ **www.vola.dk**

Wall-fixed white kitchen units □
www.boffi.com

Kitchen drama
by Ann Boyd Design
email: ann@annboyd-design.co.uk

The fashion-designer owner of this extremely grand 1870's home is a great host and loves to cook. The kitchen occupies what was originally a bedroom. Because the house is historically important, all original ornate detailing with pretty mouldings had to remain intact and untouched. The client's brief was for generous work surfaces and a sociable space where he could talk to his guests while preparing the food. He wanted the room to combine modern kitchen fittings with his collection of antiques including the crystal chandelier and Elizabethan portrait along with an old Irish oak table and chairs.

1 An antique iron and crystal chandelier makes an interesting contrast with the contemporary style of kitchen. Among makers of contemporary-style pendant lamps are Louis Poulsen □ **www.louis-poulsen.com** □ and Flos □ **www.flos.net** □ More traditional glass pendants made with world-famous Murano glass can be found at □ **www.glasschandeliers.com**

2 On the wall are cast metal mast lights from a traditional chandlers shop, they cast a powerful downlight. Among makers of such traditional ship's lighting is □ **www.davey.co.uk**

3 Vario toaster (1946) by Max Gort-Barten □ **www.dualit.com**

4 The island unit has a particularly beautiful stainless steel top with integral sink, the unit comprises a sheer, inbuilt hob, and two dishwashers. The system has white acrylic doors □ **www.boffi.com**

5 Measuring 200mm wide, the floor is finished in natural oak planks. The wide boards complement the room's generous proportions □ **for wood flooring, see the Directory of Suppliers on pages 152–55**

Triflow Doric by Franke
□ **www.franke.com**

Tara Classic by Sieger Design
□ **www.dornbracht.com**

Model No. MF2 by Smeg
□ **www.smeg.it**

Qube Sink Mixer by Bristan
□ **www.bristan.com**

Minta by Grohe
□ **www.grohe.com**

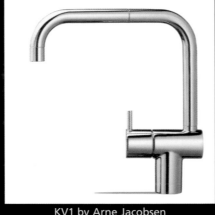

KV1 by Arne Jacobsen
□ **www.vola.dk**

HV1 by Arne Jacobsen
□ **www.vola.dk**

Tara wall-mounted by Sieger Design
□ **www.dornbracht.com**

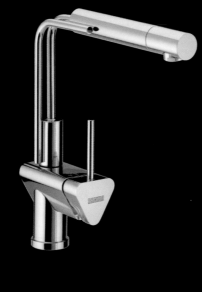

Fusion Sink Mixer by Bristan
□ **www.bristan.com**

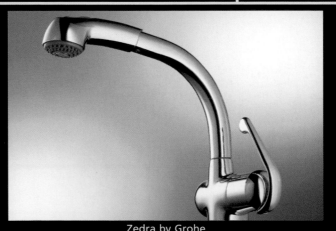

Zedra by Grohe
□ **www.grohe.com**

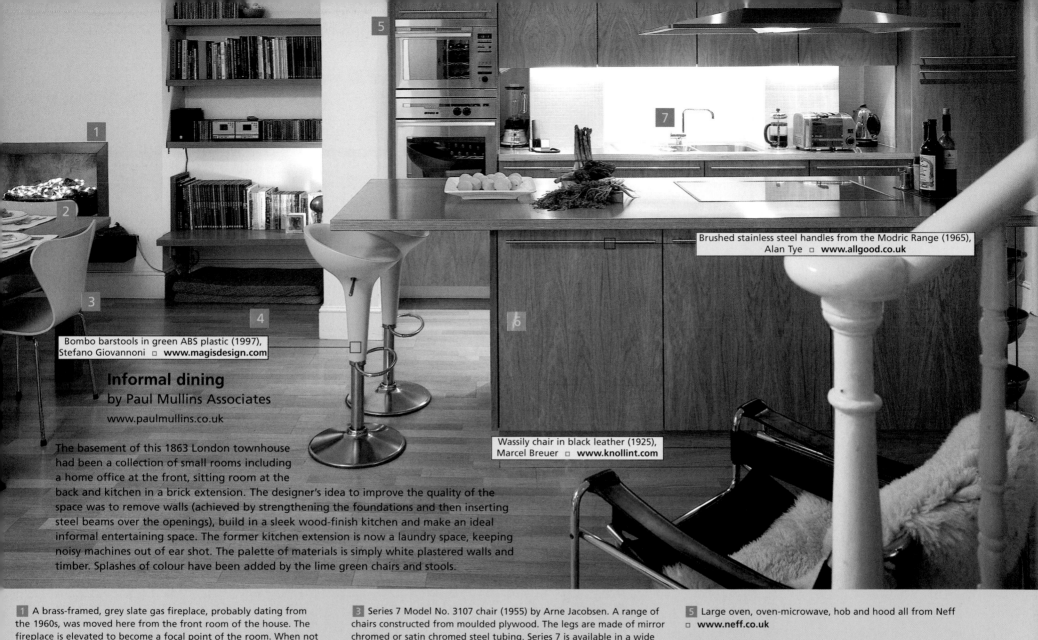

Brushed stainless steel handles from the Modric Range (1965), Alan Tye □ www.allgood.co.uk

Bombo barstools in green ABS plastic (1997), Stefano Giovannoni □ www.magisdesign.com

Informal dining
by Paul Mullins Associates

www.paulmullins.co.uk

The basement of this 1863 London townhouse had been a collection of small rooms including a home office at the front, sitting room at the back and kitchen in a brick extension. The designer's idea to improve the quality of the space was to remove walls (achieved by strengthening the foundations and then inserting steel beams over the openings), build in a sleek wood-finish kitchen and make an ideal informal entertaining space. The former kitchen extension is now a laundry space, keeping noisy machines out of ear shot. The palette of materials is simply white plastered walls and timber. Splashes of colour have been added by the lime green chairs and stools.

Wassily chair in black leather (1925), Marcel Breuer □ www.knollint.com

1 A brass-framed, grey slate gas fireplace, probably dating from the 1960s, was moved here from the front room of the house. The fireplace is elevated to become a focal point of the room. When not in use, it is filled with a string of sparkling white Christmas tree lights □ **for architectural salvage, including fireplaces, see the Directory of Suppliers on pages 152–55**

2 Bespoke solid oak dining table, 2.4m in length, designed by Paul Mullins □ **www.paulmullins.co.uk**

3 Series 7 Model No. 3107 chair (1955) by Arne Jacobsen. A range of chairs constructed from moulded plywood. The legs are made of mirror chromed or satin chromed steel tubing. Series 7 is available in a wide range of lacquer or lazur colours, as well as in natural veneers: maple, beech, ash, cherry and nut. The series includes chairs with arms, swivel chairs on castors and a pedestal chair plus a string of accessories □ **www.fritzhansen.com**

4 A hardwearing, prefinished oak flooring system. It proved to be ideal in an older property as it is flexible enough to fit where floors are not even or level □ **for wood flooring, see the Directory of Suppliers on pages 152–55**

5 Large oven, oven-microwave, hob and hood all from Neff □ **www.neff.co.uk**

6 Bespoke oak kitchen with a ply and stainless steel worktop designed by Paul Mullins □ **www.paulmullins.co.uk**

7 KV1 one-handle mixer kitchen tap (1969) by Arne Jacobsen. □ **www.vola.com**

Canned Light (2003) by Ingo Maurer
▫ **www.ingo-maurer.com**

172 (1969–78) by Poul Christiansen
▫ **www.leklint.com**

Snowball (1960) by Poul Henningsen
▫ **www.louis-poulsen.com**

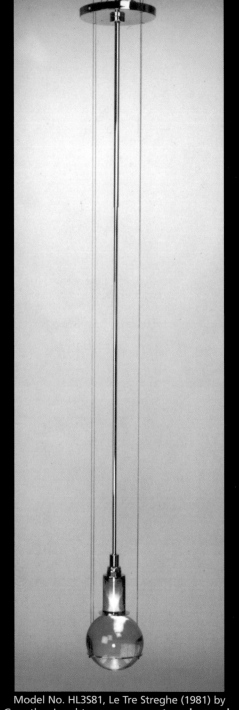

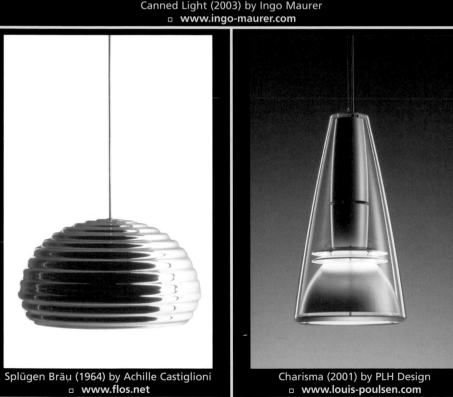

Splügen Bräu (1964) by Achille Castiglioni
▫ **www.flos.net**

Charisma (2001) by PLH Design
▫ **www.louis-poulsen.com**

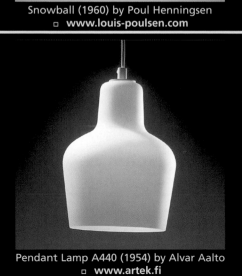

Pendant Lamp A440 (1954) by Alvar Aalto
▫ **www.artek.fi**

Model No. HL3S81, Le Tre Streghe (1981) by
Guenther Leuchtmann ▫ **www.tecnolumen.de**

Cina, Rodolfo Dordoni (now discontinued),
for similar see □ **www.flos.net**

Light touch
by Ash Sakula Architects

www.ashsak.com

The key to this design was to respect the character of the room; it is large and high-ceilinged with a bay window overlooking the rear garden. Before it was bought by its current owners, this nineteenth-century townhouse had been chopped up for multiple occupancy and divided crudely into separate dwellings. Their task was to restore the place back to a family dwelling. In the large bay window sits the dining table, and flanking the window on the other side is a pair of fridge-freezers. Meanwhile the kitchen has been stowed away as simply as possible with a run of cupboards and accessories plus an island unit. The wall-fixed units are finished in an incredibly tough white material, while the island units feature aluminium drawers.

1 Bespoke kitchen units are tailor-made to fit the space. The doors are finished with WISA-Van, a highly durable panel material set on plywood, more usually to be found lining delivery vans, which is a weather and impact resistant polyester glassfibre resin □ **www.wisa.upm-kymmene.com**

2 Bespoke stainless steel kitchen sink and work surface, which creates one continuous, and hygienic, run □ **for kitchen furniture, see the Directory of Suppliers on pages 152–55**

3 The island unit has an iroko worktop and drawers fronted with reeded aluminium. Behind here are shelves for large and awkward kitchen items. Most exciting of all, this unit also features underneath lighting that gives the unit an ethereal quality and makes it appear to float in space □ **for lighting, see the Directory of Suppliers on pages 152–55**

4 Solid maple floorboards are used for a warm but light-coloured and durable finish □ **for wood flooring, see the Directory of Suppliers on pages 152–55**

5 In addition to the two pendant lamps the kitchen features small pools of task lighting – low voltage lamps have been used around the sink area and are concealed behind the magnet message board. More small fittings are used in an interesting way under the shelving. For contemporary light fittings see Erco □ **www.erco.com** □ and Wila □ **www.wila.com**

- plastic and glass-fibre baths were once considered cheap and nasty, but the latest acrylic models are becoming popular amongst those who prefer to avoid cold metal bath sides; spa and whirlpool models are also gaining favour

- for anyone who enjoys showering, a power shower is a must, so make sure your water system is suitable; shower post systems with jets to spray the whole body are also gaining favour

- counter-top basins are stylish; glass and steel basins require regular cleaning to keep them looking their best

- good-quality, stylish taps can transform an economy suite

- if children or elderly people use the bathroom, build in handles and non-slip surfaces

- some storage is useful for cleaning materials, toilet rolls and cosmetics: store medicines in a lockable cupboard

No longer just a purely functional space, there is a fresh emphasis on the bathroom as a place of relaxation and renewal. The bathroom's new elevated status can be measured by the amount of space we are prepared to devote to it. It is quite routine for main bedrooms to have a bathroom en suite, for adults and children to have separate bathrooms, for spare bedrooms to be transformed into wetrooms and for spaces to be carved out to make extra showers and separate loos. Among the greatest influences on the new-look is the hotel bathroom. Hotel designers are not just inspiring space engineers, they have also devised ways of adding an ever-greater sense of luxury. Among the most luxurious touches are large, powerful showers, steam rooms and fully-tiled wet-room spaces, whirlpool baths, floor-to-ceiling tiling – especially marble – and pairs of wash basins. Added to this are high-quality controllable lighting and in-built music speakers. When planning a new bathroom, consider who will be using the space and how they like to wash – an early morning shower user who prefers an invigorating start to the day or an evening bath taker who wants to relax and unwind. Children and old people may need to be catered for, too, by making sure there are secure handles to aid movement, no sharp corners and non-slip surfaces.

BATHROOMS

Woodline 2 (2002) by Giampaolo Benedini
□ **www.agapedesign.it**

Newson (2003) by Marc Newson
□ **www.art-design-sculpture.co.uk**

Classic by Kaldewei
□ **www.kaldewei.com**

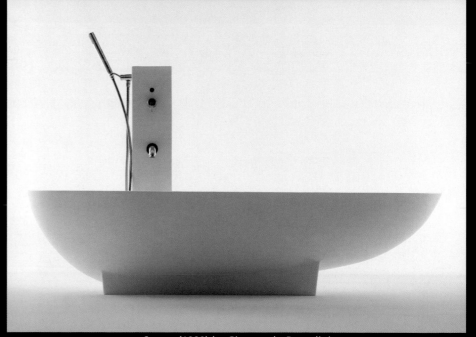

Spoon (1999) by Giampaolo Benedini
□ **www.agapedesign.it**

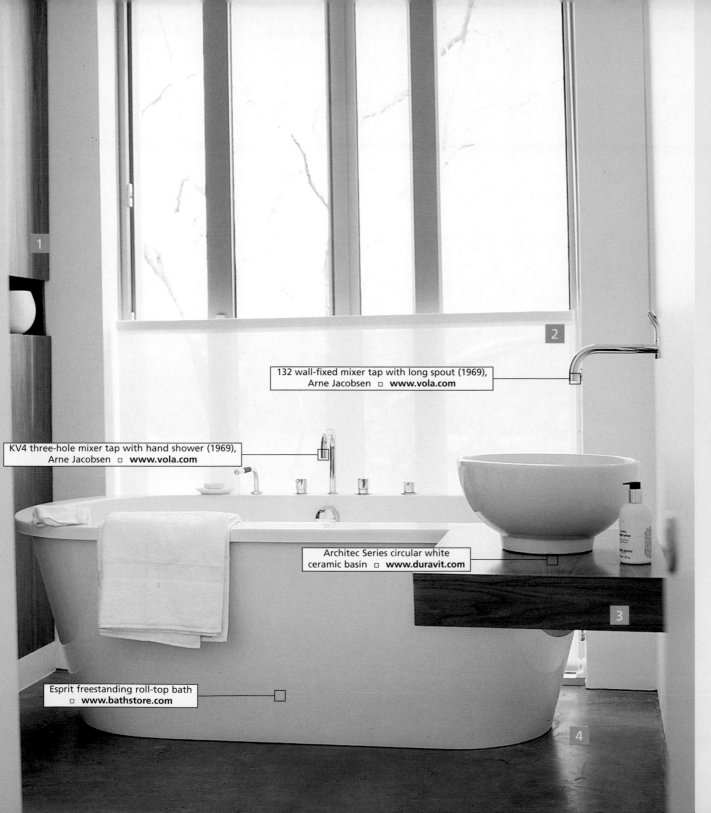

1

2

132 wall-fixed mixer tap with long spout (1969),
Arne Jacobsen □ **www.vola.com**

KV4 three-hole mixer tap with hand shower (1969),
Arne Jacobsen □ **www.vola.com**

Architec Series circular white
ceramic basin □ **www.duravit.com**

3

Esprit freestanding roll-top bath
□ **www.bathstore.com**

4

Bathroom with a view
by Denton Corker Marshall Architects
www.dcm-group.com

While most bathrooms have small windows or none at all, this has an entire wall of floor-to-ceiling glass and is a room with a view. With almost monastic simplicity the freestanding bath is complemented by the white ceramic basin sitting on its timber shelf. The blind is an ingenious detail – pull it up for modesty's sake as you climb into the bath, then, once in, it can be lowered and the window opened to enjoy the view over the local park.

1 In-built walnut wood storage space designed by the architect □ **www.dcm-group.com**

2 Smart blind designed to be pulled upwards. The screen can be in place while the bather climbs into the bath and then lowered for views over the park □ **for blinds, see the Directory of Suppliers on pages 152–55**

3 Walnut wood shelf, which ties in with the storage unit, designed by the architect □ **www.dcm-group.com**

4 The surface of the solid concrete floor has been ground to a smooth and polished finish □ **for concrete flooring, see the Directory of Suppliers on pages 152–55**

Happy D. (1999) by Sieger Design
□ **www.duravit.com**

Mood (2000) by Mårten Claesson, Eero Koivisto & Ola Rune
□ **www.boffi.com**

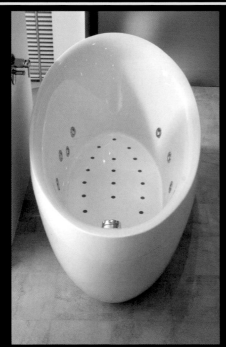

Starck 3 Rectangular Bath (2002) by
Philippe Starck □ **www.duravit.com**

Aveo by Conran & Partners
□ **www.villeroy-boch.com**

Soikko by Durat
□ **www.durat.com**

Tara Classic wall-mounted mixer tap (1991),
Sieger Design ◻ **www.dornbracht.com**

I Fiumi Po solid limestone bath (1999),
Claudio Silvestrin ◻ **www.boffi.com**

Tara Classic mixer tap with shower head (1991),
Sieger Design ◻ **www.dornbracht.com**

Pool of calm
by Claesson Koivisto Rune
www.claesson-koivisto-rune.se

Like bathing in a rockpool, this freestanding oval bath has a magical quality. It takes centre stage in the bathroom of this refurbished grand city-centre apartment where the architects wanted to create as oasis of calm for bathing and resting. Because of its tremendous weight, however, the floor of this third-floor apartment had to be strengthened with steel before the bath could be craned into place through a window. This room is the height of luxury, along with the smooth, limestone bath and sandstone floor there is an in-built, walnut-clad sauna room. The use of natural materials and neutral colours ensures this is a tranquil place.

1 Tiny ceiling-recessed low-voltage halogen light fittings are supplemented by this intriguing light set into the base of a wall niche. There's a monastic feel to this feature which is entirely in tune with the minimalism of the room ◻ **for lighting, see the Directory of Suppliers on pages 152–55**

2 Bespoke tubular steel towel rail designed by the architects, Mårten Claesson, Eero Koivisto and Ola Rune. A contemporary interpretation of the traditional wood towel rail, it is related to Beckham, the larger. tubular steel clothes hanging rail also designed by the architects ◻ **www.david.se**

3 Bespoke wall-fixed, walnut wood cabinet designed by the architects. It provides storage space and holds the basin ◻ **www.claesson-koivisto-rune.se**

4 Off-white ceramic mosaic tiles. The tiny squares complement the geometry of the room's other finishes and fittings – rectangular storage units, square floor tiles and the oval bath ◻ **for tiles, see the Directory of Suppliers on pages 152–55**

5 Swedish Gotland sandstone flooring in square tiles, which has been sealed to prevent staining by water ◻ **for stone flooring, see the Directory of Suppliers on pages 152–55**

Viceversa by Benedini Associati
□ **www.agapedesign.it**

Il Bagno by Stefano Giovannoni
□ **www.ilbagno.alessi.com**

Vaioduo Oval by Kaldewei
□ **www.kaldewei.com**

Starck 1 Oval Bath by Philippe Starck
□ **www.duravit.com**

Come on in
by Rahel Belatchew Lerdell
www.rbarchitecture.com

An inviting bath tub with picture window. This room is on the ground floor of a contemporary-style, new timber-built home which has been constructed on a difficult sloping, rocky hillside. The conventional floorplan of a house has been transposed, with the main living area positioned upstairs to make best use of natural sunlight and views. The ground floor is quiet and private. This bathroom is not overlooked. It is simple but comfortable, featuring an inviting double-ended bath, wall niches for candles, and soft towels close at hand.

1 Called Floor, these extra-long rectangular white ceramic tiles are extremely handsome and slightly reminiscent of igloo packed snow. However, despite being all white, the room feels serene rather than chilly. In contrast with the wall tiles, the floor is finished in the same style of tile, but they are brown-black in colour □ **www.ascot.it**

2 0829 aluminium door knob □ **www.fsb.de**

INXX mixer tap with chrome finish
□ **www.moraarmatur.se**

Tonga double-ended bath with central taps set in a tiled surround □ **www.sanycces.es**

Minuetto (2002) by Benedini Associati
□ **www.agapedesign.it**

Drop-in Basin by Stefano Giovannoni
□ **www.ilbagno.alessi.com**

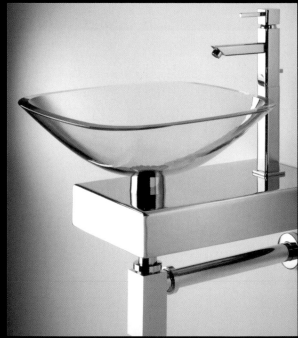

Glass Bowl by Avante
□ **www.avantebathrooms.com**

Starck 1 Washbasin by Philippe Starck
□ **www.duravit.com**

Foster Washbasin with Pedestal (1999) by Norman Foster
□ **www.duravit.com**

Tara fixed showerhead with mixer controls and hand-held attachment (1991), Sieger Design □ **www.dornbracht.com**

Tara wall-mounted mixer tap (1991), Sieger Design □ **www.dornbracht.com**

Scola white ceramic basin
□ **www.duravit.com**

Pooled resources
by Project Orange
www.projectorange.com

Instead of opting for a separate en suite bathroom away from their children, the clients for this project wanted a large bathroom that could be shared by the whole family. The generous space has given them room for a pair of large wash basins and a luxurious double shower, as seen in the mirror reflection, which is bathed in plenty of natural sunlight pouring through the acid-etched glass rooflight. Two clear glass circles in this rooflight provide views of the sky. For an added sense of luxury, and to reduce its impact on the room, the bath has been sunk into the floor and the room is lined with stone.

1 Unusually, the floor and walls have been lined with Sera blue limestone. This gives the room a wonderful sheer finish and tranquil feel □ **for stone flooring, see the Directory of Suppliers on pages 152–55**

2 Recessed square wall lights called Side are used throughout this room, above the toilet and bidet, and built into the top of the wall around the skylight □ **www.kreon.com**

3 A neat doubled-ended white bath with central tap, set into the ground. By lowering the level of the bath, this clever design device makes it seem more luxurious and has the added benefit of reducing the tub's visual impact on the room □ **www.duravit.com**

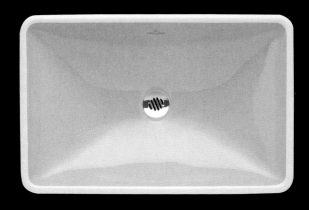

Viceversa by Benedini Associati
□ **www.agapedesign.it**

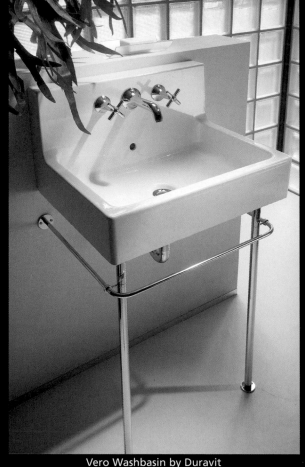

Starck 1 Bowl by Philippe Starck
□ **www.duravit.com**

Vero Washbasin by Duravit
□ **www.duravit.com**

Colorline Rectangular Basin by Villeroy & Boch
□ **www.villeroy-boch.com**

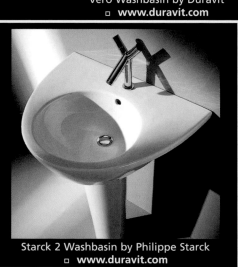

Natural Stone Model 14 by Avante
□ **www.avantebathrooms.com**

Starck 2 Washbasin by Philippe Starck
□ **www.duravit.com**

Wall-fixed, double-arm illuminated magnifying mirror in chrome □ www.samuel-heath.com

Aria white ceramic basic □ www.bathstore.com

As nature intended
by Phil Simmons at Simmons Interiors
www.simmonsinteriors.com

A minimalist interior incorporating dramatic lighting and textures was the brief for the refurbishment of this bathroom and entire riverside apartment. Materials used throughout the home are luxurious, from the curved glass wall and limestone floor at the entrance, the bespoke cherry wood furniture and fitted cupboards in the bedroom to the cherry wood and stainless steel kitchen. The bathroom is equally plush with its neat pair of countertop basins, sitting on a stone bench, limestone clad walls and teak flooring.

1 Square, ceiling-recessed downlighters
□ www.deltalight.com

2 Fittings to glass door to room and shower screen
□ www.dorma.com

3 Space three-piece wall-mounted mixer taps with chrome spout □ www.bathstore.com

4 Myson MRR4 chrome towel rail
□ www.myson.co.uk

5 Limestone wall tiles. When using stone in bathrooms and kitchens always check with the supplier for advice on appropriate finishes to prevent staining □ for tiles, see the Directory of Suppliers on pages 152–55

6 Flooring under the basins in Elterwater cumbrian stone, a green stone with lighter coloured veining □ for stone flooring, see the Directory of Suppliers on pages 152–55

7 Zero Light WC, wall-hung pan and heavy duty white seat □ www.bathstore.com

8 Floor-inset circular uplighters □ www.deltalight.com

9 Teak floor in a slatted design □ for wood flooring, see the Directory of Suppliers on pages 152–55

Starck 1 Washbasin by Philippe Starck
□ **www.duravit.com**

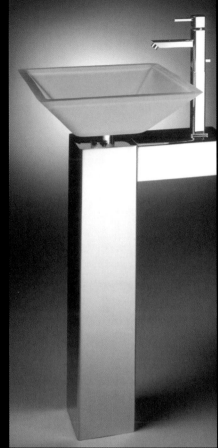

Square Bowl by Avante
□ **www.avantebathrooms.com**

Dreamscape Washbasin by Duravit
□ **www.duravit.com**

Colorline Square Basin by Villeroy & Boch
□ **www.villeroy-boch.com**

Colorline Triangular Basin by Villeroy & Boch
□ **www.villeroy-boch.com**

Natural Stone Model 13 by Avante
□ **www.avantebathrooms.com**

Metropole Basin by Christo Lefroy Brooks
□ **www.lefroybrooks.com**

Happy D. (1999) by Sieger Design
□ **www.duravit.com**

Wall-fixed extending mirror in chrome
□ **www.samuel-heath.com**

Axor Starck Widespread Set,
Philippe Starck □ **www.hansgrohe.com**

Stainless steel circular basin
□ **www.agapedesign.it**

A machine for bathing
by Groupe l'Arche with
Wessel von Loringhoven of CasaNova
email: archeplan@larche.ch

During the refurbishment of his home, the client commissioned the architect to create a tough, masculine style of bathroom with a splash of luxury. Rich stone and timber are used to line the space and make a de luxe cabin. Alongside these very obviously natural materials, complete with their grain and vein, a finely tuned industrial aesthetic is added with the exquisitely machined pair of stainless-steel basins and taps, the tall, vertical radiator and the smaller accessories, including the extending mirror and towel rail.

1 Green granite with a delicate white vein is used to line walls and stand as the bath side panel. Granite is an extremely tough stone, available around the world □ **for tiles, see the Directory of Suppliers on pages 152–55**

2 Stainless steel vertical radiator, ideal for warming bath towels. For similar radiators see Zehnder □ **www.zehnder.ws** □ and Imperial □ **www.imperialtowelrails.com**

3 Holes have been drilled into the granite partly for decoration but also to encourage air circulation, essential in the damp atmosphere of a bathroom □ **for tiles, see the Directory of Suppliers on pages 152–55**

4 Teak – a traditional material for ships decking because of its durability, especially when exposed to water – is used for flooring and appears again on the walls, this time used vertically to frame the inbuilt cabinets □ **for wood flooring, see the Directory of Suppliers on pages 152–55**

Tara Basin Bridge Mixer by Sieger Design
□ **www.dornbracht.com**

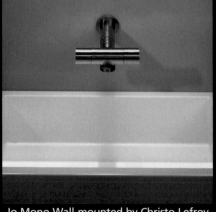

Jo Mono Basin by Christo Lefroy Brooks
□ **www.lefroybrooks.com**

Murano Waterfall by Hansa
□ **www.hansa.de**

Axor Starck Mixer by Philippe Starck
□ **www.hansgrohe.com**

Circa 29 Pillar Taps by Sottini
□ **www.sottini.co.uk**

Jo Mono Wall-mounted by Christo Lefroy
Brooks □ **www.lefroybrooks.com**

Axor Starck Puro Mixer by Philippe Starck
□ **www.hansgrohe.com**

Tara Basin Mixer by Sieger Design
□ **www.dornbracht.com**

Atrio High Bowl Mixer by Grohe
□ **www.grohe.com**

Alchemy Dual Control Basin Mixer by
Sottini □ **www.sottini.co.uk**

KV10 three-hole mixer taps,
Arne Jacobsen □ **www.vola.dk**

Light fantastic
by Jean Nouvel
www.jeannouvel.fr

Since many of the best ideas for bathrooms at home are drawn from bathrooms in hotels, this is an inspiring guest bathroom in a Swiss hotel, called The Hotel, designed by Jean Nouvel. The design is conceived to 'celebrate simplicity and spirituality as much as it does elegance and refinement. The central idea is to create something quite unlike anything before that provides guests with a magical, exciting and unforgettable feeling.' The bathroom is dark and womb-like with light concentrated around the washbasin and mirror area. The lights set into the mirror are reminiscent of theatrical changing rooms.

1 Indirect light to the ceiling by compact fluorescent tube hidden behind a mirror-finish aluminium panel. This type of lamp is widely available and produced by all big-name lamp manufacturers □ **for lighting, see the Directory of Suppliers on pages 152–55**

2 A bespoke design, which sets a quartet of oversize light bulbs at the corners of this mirror □ **for lighting, see the Directory of Suppliers on pages 152–55**

3 A range of stainless steel accessories, including the door handle □ **www.dline.com**

4 Bespoke countertop by Jean Nouvel with integral basins in Corian □ **www.corian.com**

5 The flooring combines reconstituted stone tiles called Silestone white □ **www.silestone.com** and jatoba wood, also known as Brazilian cherry □ **for wood flooring, see the Directory of Suppliers on pages 152–55**

Bath and Shower Tap by Stefano Giovannoni
□ **www.ilbagno.alessi.com**

Axor Citterio Trim Tub Set by
Antonio Citterio □ **www.hansgrohe.com**

Floor-standing Bath Tap by Stefano Giovannoni
□ **www.ilbagno.alessi.com**

Elle Wall-mounted Bath Tap by Bonomi
□ **www.bonomi.it**

Alchemy Standpipes Bath Filler by Sottini
□ **www.art-design-sculpture.co.uk**

Elle Bath Tap by Bonomi
□ **www.bonomi.it**

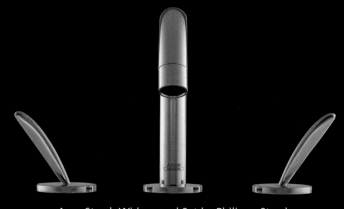

Axor Starck Widespread Set by Philippe Starck
□ **www.hansgrohe.com**

Tara Classic mixer tap (1991),
Sieger Design □ **www.dornbracht.com**

Tara Classic mixer tap (1991),
Sieger Design □ **www.dornbracht.com**

Centroform Oval double-ended steel bath with central
plughole □ **www.kaldewei.com**

Starck 1 series white ceramic basin,
Philippe Starck □ **www.duravit.com**

Fluid space
by Form Design Architecture

www.form-architecture.co.uk

When the owner took over this penthouse it was an awkward-shaped shell: from the difficult spaces, the architect created an intriguing apartment of flowing spaces, each with a distinct character. The bathroom is sited in the mezzanine level next to the main bedroom, a haven away from the formal, public spaces below. The idea was to create an interesting space with beautiful, luxurious finishes. The double shower with fibre optics is inspired – bathing the user with light as well as water.

1 Bespoke shower designed by the architect. The shower rose incorporates fibre optics to bathe the user in light as well as water □ **www.form-architecture.co.uk** □ This spacious double shower runs along the wall opposite the bath and basins and has a glass screen □ **for architectural glass, see the Directory of Suppliers on pages 152–55**

2 Ceiling-recessed low-voltage halogen lamps. The crisp quality of light from these lamps is excellent in bathrooms where it adds sparkle to the reflective surfaces □ **for lighting, see the Directory of Suppliers on pages 152–55**

3 Whatever the mood, this bathroom is wired for sound with speakers from the home's fully integrated sound system that are concealed within the ceiling □ **www.bwspeakers.com**

4 Wall-mounted shower control □ **for bathroom fittings, see the Directory of Suppliers on pages 152–55**

5 A single length of Bateige Blue limestone ingeniously serves as the surround for the bath as well as the counter top for the pair of matching white ceramic basins. Two recesses are lined with metal laminate for towel storage. The stone was sealed to make it waterproof □ **for stone tiles, see the Directory of Suppliers on pages 152–55**

6 Limestone floor tiles, treated with a water sealant recommended by the manufacturer □ **www.lithofin.de**

7 The sliding mirrored doors double as shutters to the window over the bath, and doors to the medicine cabinets either side when open.

Amera Shower System by Grohe
□ **www.grohe.com**

Rainshower by Grohe
□ **www.grohe.com**

Axor Citterio Showerhead by Antonio Citterio
□ **www.hansgrohe.com**

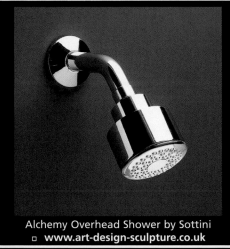

Alchemy Overhead Shower by Sottini
□ **www.art-design-sculpture.co.uk**

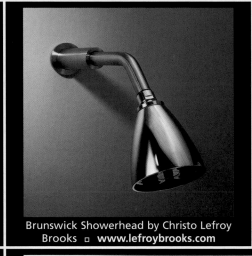

Brunswick Showerhead by Christo Lefroy
Brooks □ **www.lefroybrooks.com**

Jo Headset Shower by Christo Lefroy
Brooks □ **www.lefroybrooks.com**

Jo Wall-mounted Shower by Christo
Lefroy Brooks □ **www.lefroybrooks.com**

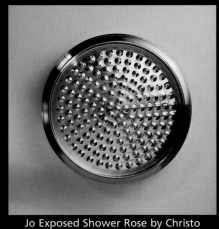

Jo Exposed Shower Rose by Christo
Lefroy Brooks □ **www.lefroybrooks.com**

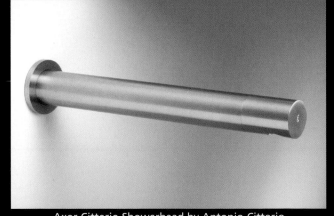

Axor Citterio Showerhead by Antonio Citterio
□ **www.hansgrohe.com**

classic rose showerhead, for similar see
▫ **www.grohe.com**

1

ma ISOMIX thermostatic mixer in chrome
▫ **www.rubinetteriestella.it**

Emisfero wall-mounted mixer tap in chrome
▫ **www.rubinetteriestella.it**

Towel Rail 960 in chrome
▫ **www.rubinetteriestella.it**

2

3

4

A bigger splash
by Philippe Starck
www.philippe-starck.com

For anyone who loves showers, this is the perfect place for washing and pampering – a floor-to-ceiling, fully tiled wetroom. The huge showerheads guarantee a powerful and invigorating shower experience. Free from the constraints of pokey shower cubicles, and with twin showers and twin basins, there's even enough room to share the space with a friend. Unusually for a bathroom, the colour scheme includes splashes of red.

1 Large-scale 50 x 50mm black mosaic tiles have been used to line this wetroom from floor to ceiling ▫ **www.winckelmans.com**

2 Roma tumbler holder in chrome with transparent glass tumbler ▫ **www.rubinetteriestella.it**

3 White ceramic square basin ▫ **www.duravit.com**

4 Stool made in stone ▫ **www.habitat.net**

Double-sided Make-up Mirror by Keuco
▫ **www.keuco.de**

Soap Dish by Keuco
▫ **www.keuco.de**

Open Holder by Keuco
▫ **www.keuco.de**

Qube Roll Holder by Bristan
▫ **www.bristan.com**

Axor Starck Towel Hook by
Philippe Starck ▫ **www.hansgrohe.com**

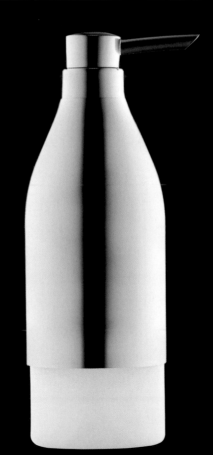

COM601 by Stefano Giovannoni
▫ **www.agapedesign.it**

Qube Tumbler by Bristan
▫ **www.bristan.com**

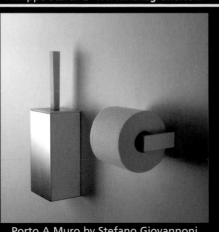

Porto A Muro by Stefano Giovannoni
▫ **www.agapedesign.it**

Axor Starck by Philippe Starck
▫ **www.hansgrohe.com**

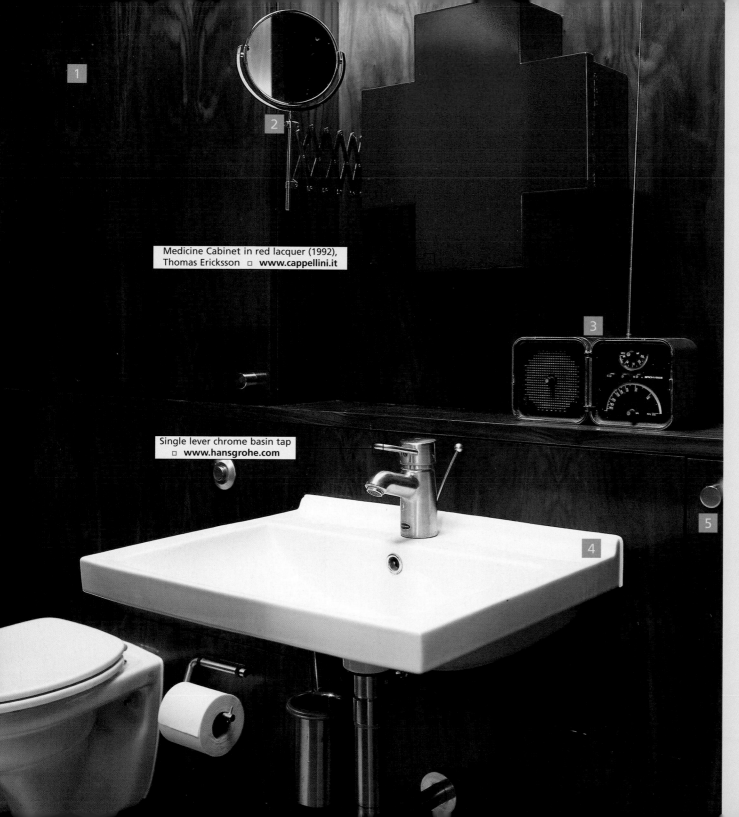

Medicine Cabinet in red lacquer (1992),
Thomas Ericksson □ **www.cappellini.it**

Single lever chrome basin tap
□ **www.hansgrohe.com**

Class cabin
by Simon Allford of
Allford Hall Monaghan Morris
www.ahmm.co.uk

A cabin-style, walnut-lined bathroom continues
the design theme in this remodelled flat, which
is as classy as the A-deck cabins of a luxury liner.
The bathroom is compact but luxuriously
finished. The use of dark, richly patterned walnut
wood to line the walls is an unusual and
refreshing choice when light coloured bathrooms
are the norm. Cork flooring tiles, which are
readily available from all good flooring stores,
are sealed with a water- and stainproof acrylic
finish. Cork flooring enjoyed a heyday in the
1970s, but is used less often now, however it is a
natural and sustainable material that is warm to
the touch and extremely hardwearing.

1 Walnut cladding □ **for wood, including cladding,
see the Directory of Suppliers on pages 152–55**

2 Wall-fixed extending and pivoting mirror in chrome
□ **www.samuel-heath.com**

3 An original Brionvega ts522 portable radio by
Marco Zanussi and Richard Sapper. A classic 1960s design
□ **www.brionvega.it**

4 Smart, rectangular-shaped, wall-mounted, white
ceramic basin which suits the masculine, clubby look
of this bathroom. Classic ranges can be found in the
products by Laufen □ **www.laufen.com**

5 Cabinet door knob Modric 2501 in brushed
stainless steel □ **www.allgood.co.uk**

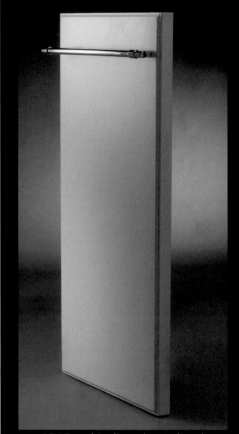

Alvita by Æstus
□ **www.aestus-radiators.com**

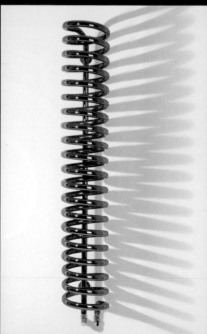

Hot Spring by Bisque
□ **www.bisque.co.uk**

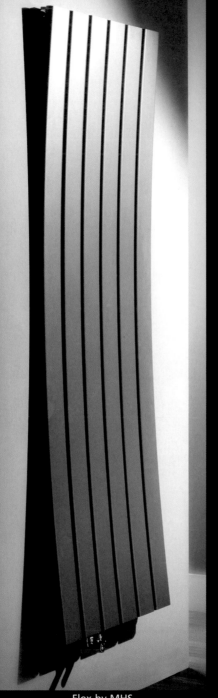

Flex by MHS
□ **www.mhsboilers.com/radiators**

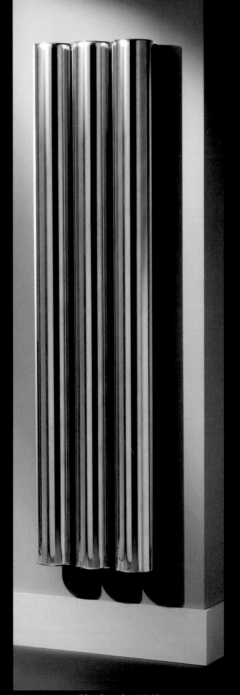

Big One by MHS
□ **www.mhsboilers.com/radiators**

P5V Towel Radiator by Hudevad
□ **www.hudevad.com**

Hot Hoop by Bisque
□ **www.bisque.co.uk**

Remodelled townhouse
by Alison Brooks Architects

www.alisonbrooksarchitects.com

During the refurbishment of this 1970's townhouse, the bathroom was opened up to adjoin the bedroom. The architect conceived the bathroom as a piece of sculpture, it sits raised up on a limestone platform and the curvy bath can be seen from the bed. Natural light falls onto the bath from a circular rooflight. Throughout the house the fitted furniture has been designed by the architect and built in cherry wood.

1 A single sheet of toughened, sandblasted 12mm glass makes an ideal shower enclosure. It looks particularly elegant because it has been set into metal channels sunk into the wall, ceiling and floor dispensing with the need to use a frame □ **for architectural glass, see the Directory of Suppliers on pages 152–55**

2 112 wall-mounted, one-handled mixer tap □ **www.vola.com**

3 BluToo plywood countertop circular basin with satin lacquer finish □ **www.minetti.de**

4 The shimmering bath surround is made in aluminium Formica, which has been laminated to a plywood backing. It is warmer to the touch than metal sheeting and doesn't attract fingermarks □ **www.formica.com**

5 Limestone flooring is best laid on a solid base, such as concrete. If laid on a wooden floor, the weight can be too great for joists and the slight movement inevitable with wooden floors can disturb the grout and allow water to seep through the floor □ **for stone flooring, see the Directory of Suppliers on pages 152–55**

Cobra-Therm wall-mounted heated towel radiator in chrome □ **www.bisque.co.uk**

BK10 one-handled mixer tap with hand shower (1959), Arne Jacobsen □ **www.vola.com**

Megaform Oval double-ended steel bath with central plughole □ **www.kaldewei.com**

Hot Box by MHS
▫ **www.mhsradiators.com**

O.J.C. (1991) by Giampaolo Benedini
▫ **www.agapedesign.it**

Model No. M53280 by Stefano Giovannoni
▫ **www.ilbagno.alessi.com**

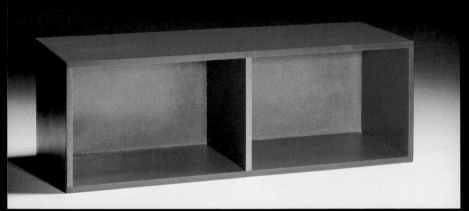

Hylly by Durat
▫ **www.durat.com**

Mirror cabinet by Keuco
▫ **www.keuco.de**

Art Deco style

by Fox Linton Associates

www.foxlinton.com

This extremely handsome bathroom was inspired by the great Art Deco period of the 1930s and uses a palette of luxurious materials, which has been chosen for its rich pattern and strong contrasting light and dark shades – a characteristic of the period design. The materials include pale limestone and dark marble, whilst the addition of glass, walnut wood for the cupboards and a glint of stainless steel on light fittings and taps adds to the richness. The design makes excellent use of space, finding room for twin basins as well as shelving for towels. Take care when purchasing bathroom lighting as different countries around the world have their own regulations. Check that any lamps match the specification before you buy.

1 Marron honed chocolate marble used on the walls and floor □ **for stone flooring, see the Directory of Suppliers on pages 152–55**

2 Wallcovering by bath is a panel of white glass, which gives a luxurious and sheer finish □ **for architectural glass, see the Directory of Suppliers on pages 152–55**

3 Tara wall-mounted mixer tap (1991) by Sieger Design. A range that not only includes taps, but also a selection of matching bathroom accessories, including storage units, soap holders and mirrors □ **www.dornbracht.com**

4 Bespoke limestone countertop circular basin □ **for bathroom furniture, see the Directory of Suppliers on pages 152–55**

5 Bespoke countertop in otto beige limestone to contrast with marble used on the walls and floor □ **for stone worktops, see the Directory of Suppliers on pages 152–55**

6 Bespoke walnut under-basin storage cupboards designed by the architect □ **www.foxlinton.com**

Bespoke pendant lamp designed by the architect □ **www.foxlinton.com**

Tara wall-mounted mixer tap (1991), Sieger Design □ **www.dornbracht.com**

BetteStarlet double-ended white enamelled bath □ **www.bette.de**

• whether it's a Victorian iron bedstead or a minimal plinth, the style of bed will set the character for the room

• we own more clothes and shoes than any previous generation. Unless you are incredibly rigorous at recycling unwanted clothes, when planning new cupboards, always overestimate your needs by around 20 percent

• take great care in selecting a mattress and buy the best

quality that you can afford. Pocket sprung designs are extremely comfortable

• a wardrobe light is simple to achieve and so useful when it comes to finding just the right shirt or jacket

• if daylight interrupts your sleep, fit a black-out blind to the inside of the window

• build in good lighting, around mirrors for dressing and for reading in bed

whether opting for the uncluttered calm of minimalism or the reassuring cosiness of a more traditionally furnished space, the bedroom should be restful and comfortable. The bed is a major element, which needs to be chosen with care. A good quality mattress may not be a thing of beauty, but the very best firm and pocket-

hotels where the emphasis is on making the most of sensual, natural materials such as timber flooring, deep pile rugs, gorgeous linen, soft blankets and velvet throws. However, while it is associated with sleep, for most of us the bedroom is a multi-functional space used for storing clothes, dressing and making up, watching television,

BEDROOMS

sprung types will be a joy to sleep on for years. The style of this piece of furniture will influence the look of the entire room, however it is fun to play with contrasts – a huge, dark wood, Gothic-style bed could look magnificent in an otherwise minimally furnished room. Like bathrooms, interesting ideas are often drawn from

meditating, working out and even accommodating a home office. Lighting is especially important; ambient lighting is required for early mornings and evenings, which can be achieved with pendant and/or wall lamps. However, additional lighting is needed by mirrors and is essential for reading in bed.

Model No. 1870, Alfa (2002) by Emaf Progetti
□ **www.zanotta.it**

Drift by Michael Sodeau
□ **www.twentytwentyone.com**

Aluminium Bed by Bruno Fattorini
□ **www.mdfitalia.it**

REM by Terence Woodgate
□ **www.scp.co.uk**

Bed by Jasper Morrison
□ **www.cappellini.it**

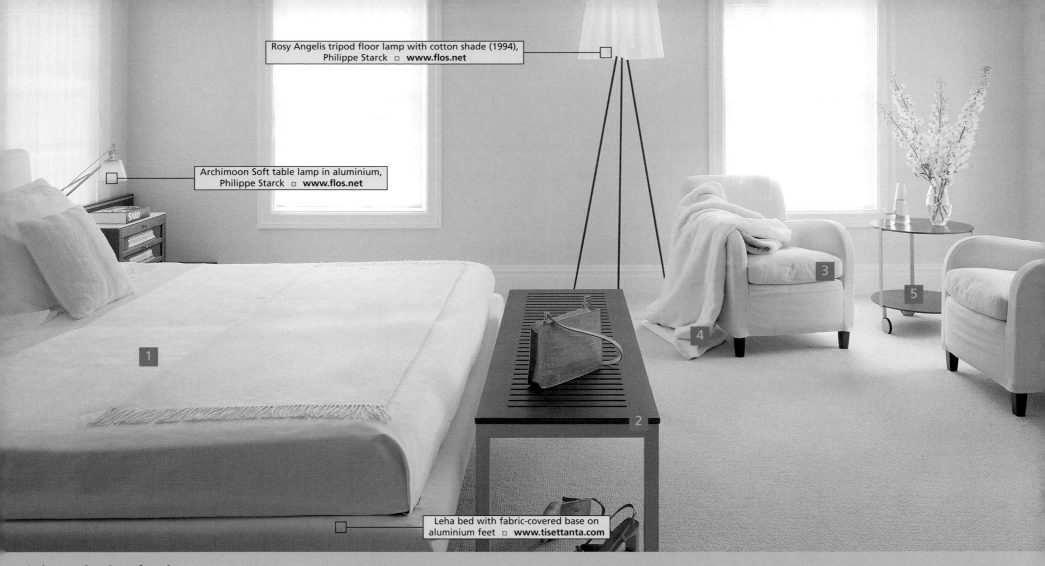

Rosy Angelis tripod floor lamp with cotton shade (1994), Philippe Starck □ **www.flos.net**

Archimoon Soft table lamp in aluminium, Philippe Starck □ **www.flos.net**

Leha bed with fabric-covered base on aluminium feet □ **www.tisettanta.com**

Lighter shade of pale
by Harry Elson Architect

www.harryelson.com

The use of pale neutral colours, soft upholstery materials and carpet, with details in natural wood have combined to make this an extremely inviting and restful bedroom. The house is built in a neo-colonial style, and in deliberate contrast with the historic look of the exterior, the recent refurbishment has provided the young owners with sophisticated, contemporary interiors. The design idea was to simplify the interiors so that the personality of each space was created through the furniture and furnishings. This main bedroom is modern classic in style.

1 Pure cotton bed linen □ **www.frette.com**

2 Lugano, a useful end of bed bench, part of the Halifax range □ **www.tisettanta.com**

3 Susanna, soft upholstered armchairs, by Vico Magistretti. They add a sense of luxury and calm to the room □ **www.depadova.it**

4 White shirred mink throw □ **www.frette.com**

5 Giro table (1997–99), by Anna Deplano. A circular two-tier, castor-mounted steel-frame table □ **www.zanotta.it**

Model No. ol2-c04, Victor by Mario Mazzer
□ **www.poliform.it**

Model No. e7, Rapsodie by Pepe Tanzi
□ **www.poliform.it**

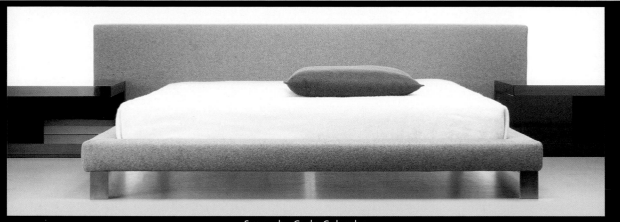

Segno by Carlo Colombo
□ **www.cappellini.it**

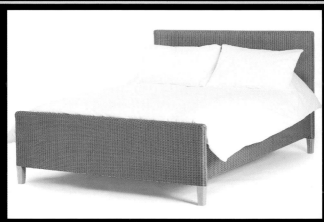

Discovery by Lloyd Loom Studio
□ **www.lloydloom.com**

Eco (2002) by Emilio Nanni
□ **www.zanotta.it**

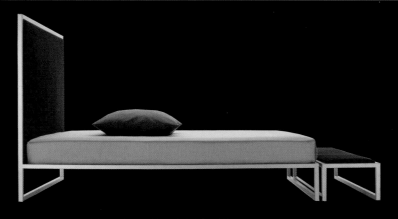

Model No. 1702, Mini (2002) by Emaf Progetti
□ **www.zanotta.it**

Low-Pad easy chair (1999) in padded white leather and chrome, Jasper Morrison □ **www.cappellini.it**

Wenge wood-frame bed with bedhead upholstered in grey moleskin felt □ **www.poliform.it**

Laid-back luxury

by Tara Bernerd of Target Living

www.targetliving.com

The brief for this bedroom was to create a 'simple and fresh-looking' scheme to reflect the contemporary style of this home. It is an elegant courtyard house by leading British architect Sir Terry Farrell where the emphasis is on transparency with huge sheets of floor-to-ceiling glass giving views into the pretty garden as well as through the whole house. The bedroom is furnished in a rich palette of materials, including leather and wenge wood, with plenty of horizontal lines – the long ottoman at the end of the bed and low-level easy chair – lending a tranquil air to the space.

1 Shashiko woven khaki cotton weave bedcover
□ **www.donghia.com**

2 Handmade cushion with shocking pink sequin border to add a splash of colour □ **for home accessories, see the Directory of Suppliers on pages 152–55**

3 Bespoke brown crocodile-print leather ottoman designed by Tara Bernerd □ **www.targetliving.com**

4 Fold-away bedside tables, 1920s Lucite Perspex. For specialists in transparent furniture see Bobo □ **www.bobodesign.co.uk**

5 Enormous white Perspex lamps. For a selection of beautiful white lamps see the Shadows collection (1999) by Marcel Wanders □ **www.cappellini.it**

6 Shashiko woven khaki cotton weave, same material as bedcover □ **www.donghia.com**

Oxygène Wardrobe System by Gautier
□ **www.gautier.fr**

Classic Linen Basket by Lloyd Loom Studio
□ **www.lloydloom.com**

BL451 (1997) by Marco Ferreri
□ **www.agapedesign.it**

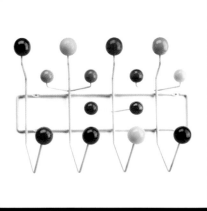

Hang-It-All (1953) by Charles & Ray Eames
□ **www.vitra.com**

Model No. po2-06, Senzafine New Entry Wardrobe by CR Poliform
□ **www.poliform.it**

Beckham (2000) by Mårten Claesson,
Eero Koivisto & Ola Rune □ **www.david.se**

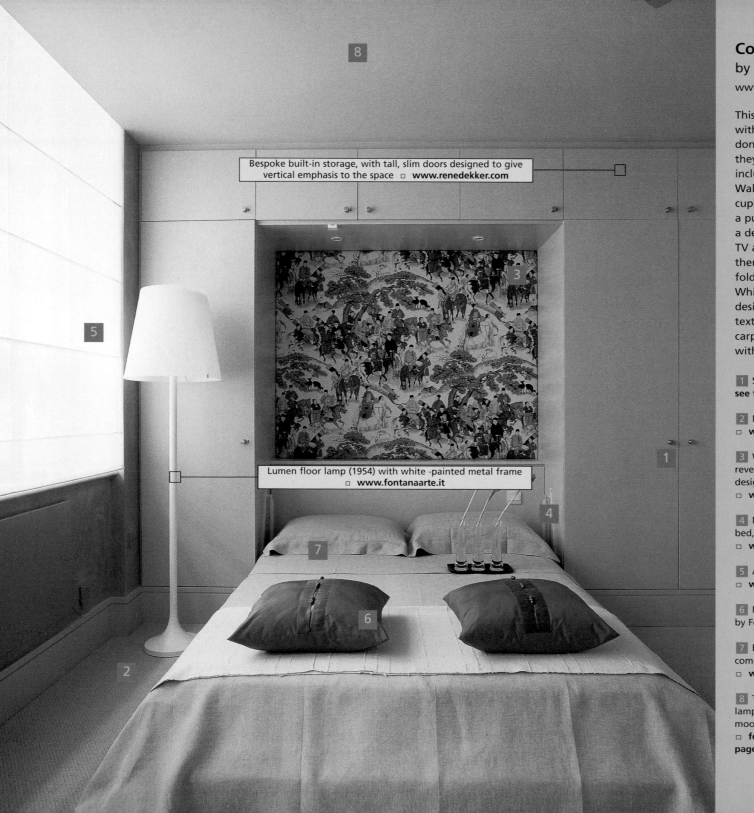

Bespoke built-in storage, with tall, slim doors designed to give vertical emphasis to the space □ **www.renedekker.com**

Lumen floor lamp (1954) with white -painted metal frame □ **www.fontanaarte.it**

Compact living
by Rene Dekker
www.renedekker.com

This small studio apartment has been designed with big ambitions. The 25 square metres of space don't just function as a well-designed living space, they also have to work hard as an office and include reference to the client's Chinese heritage. Walls are lined from floor to ceiling with cupboards; on one wall, cupboards transform into a pull-down bed. Opposite, doors open to reveal a desk with drawers, a fax machine and modem, TV and sound system. In the centre of the room there's a soft seating area, and with the bed folded up, space for a dining table and chairs. While the colour scheme is pale taupe, the designer wanted to include a range of interesting textures including polished plaster walls, soft carpet, voile Roman blinds. Zesty colour is added with rust coloured silk cushions and paintings.

1 Steel door knobs □ **for architectural ironmongery, see the Directory of Suppliers on pages 152–55**

2 Natural Rope carpet, in a colour called String □ **www.timpagecarpets.co.uk**

3 When the bed is pulled down from the wall it reveals this pretty printed fabric panel, Les Cavaliers designed by Manuel Canovas, from Colefax and Fowler □ **www.colefaxantiques.com**

4 Mechanism for raising and lowering the stowaway bed, by the architectural ironmongery expert Häfele □ **www.haefele.de**

5 A light cotton viole fabric from Nya Nordiska □ **www.nya.com**

6 Rust coloured silk made into Oriental-style cushions by Fox Linton Associates □ **www.foxlinton.com**

7 Bed linen by The Linen Mill, which has a sister company called The Leather Bed Company □ **www.thelinenmill.com**

8 Twenty ceiling-recessed, low-voltage halogen lamps were added to enable the owner to change the mood of the space with the use of dimmer switches □ **for lighting, see the Directory of Suppliers on pages 152–55**

Floorlamp A809 (1959) by Alvar Aalto
□ **www.artek.fi**

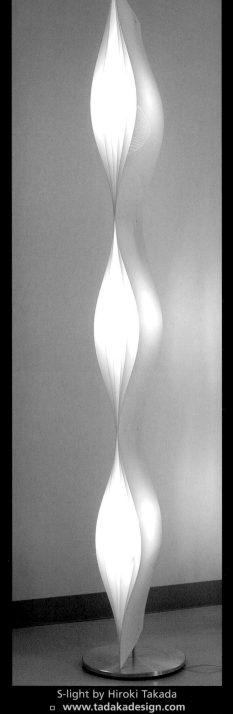

Berlin by Mårten Claesson, Eero Koivisto
& Ola Rune □ **www.atelje-lyktan.se**

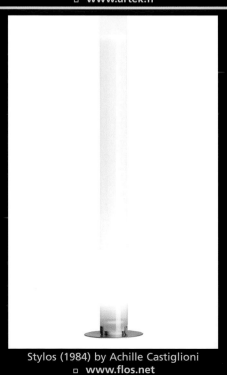

Little Big Lamp (2003) by Ingo Maurer
□ **www.ingo-maurer.com**

Roatinno (1935) by Eileen Gray
□ **www.classicon.com**

Stylos (1984) by Achille Castiglioni
□ **www.flos.net**

S-light by Hiroki Takada
□ **www.tadakadesign.com**

5

Tolomeo aluminium wall lamp (1987), Michele de Lucchi
& Giancarlo Fassina □ **www.artemide.com**

1

2

D line range, B102.0 pull handles (1970s),
Knud Holscher □ **www.dline.com**

4

3

Maly beech wood and upholstered bed with aluminium feet
and tv table (1983), Peter Maly □ **www.ligne-roset.com**

Reinvented space
by DSP Architects

www.dsparchitecture.co.uk

When the owner of this riverside apartment had the
opportunity to buy and build on the roofspace above, he
decided to make the lower part of his duplex into a luxurious
bedroom suite complete with dressing room plus a guest room.
Upstairs, a glass box addition was constructed for the new
kitchen, dining and living area. The architect installed two
beautiful bathrooms complete with spa baths, and simple,
finely detailed bedrooms. This main bedroom has glass sliding
doors to the new dressing room and French doors to the terrace.

1 Tubular steel radiator, for similar see
□ **www.hudevad.dk**

2 Solid white American Oak, tongue and groove boards, 125mm wide
and with decorative V-joint. Widely available flooring type
□ **for wood flooring, see the Directory of Suppliers on pages 152–55**

3 Toughened, acid-etched glass on Häfele Junior 80 sliding track
□ **www.haefele.de**

4 The dressing room fitted cupboards were custom designed and built
using MDF doors which have been painted with eggshell oil paint
applied by roller for a sheer finish □ **www.dsparchitecture.co.uk**

5 Unusual blinds in woven aluminium □ **for blinds, see the Directory
of Suppliers on pages 152–55**

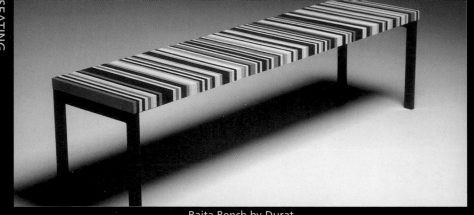

Raita Bench by Durat
□ **www.durat.com**

Fan Chair by Hiroki Takada
□ **www.tadakadesign.com**

Model No. CH28 (1951) by Hans J. Wegner
□ **www.carlhansen.com**

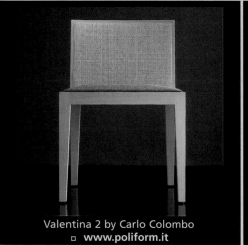

Valentina 2 by Carlo Colombo
□ **www.poliform.it**

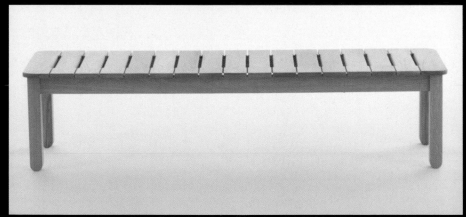

Spring Back Chair by Matthew Bear &
Scott Moulton □ **www.unionstudio.com**

Knotted Chair (1996) by Marcel Wanders
□ **www.cappellini.it**

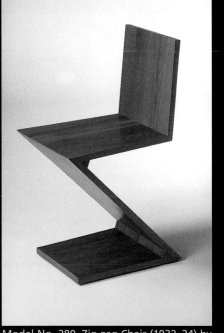

Urban Bench by Matthew Hilton
□ **www.scp.co.uk**

Model No. 280, Zig-zag Chair (1932–34) by
Gerrit Thomas Rietveld □ **www.cassina.it**

Charles bed (1998), an extension of the sofa range, Antonio Citterio □ **www.bebitalia.it**

Panton chair in red injection-moulded plastic (1960), Verner Panton □ **www.vitra.com**

Prince AHA stool in white polypropylene, Philippe Starck □ **www.kartell.it**

Period piece
by Simon Siegel

www.atomicinteriors.co.uk

For many years Simon and Monica Siegel has known about and admired this stylish Modernist house built in central England, but when it eventually came on the market the price tag was too high. However, when the potential buyer's bid fell through, they felt it was fate and made an offer that was accepted. The house was designed in the 1960s by architect David Shelley, and has survived the years pretty much intact and unscathed by fad and fashion. It is furnished with the impressive post-war furniture collection owned by Simon Siegel, who is in the interior design and retail business, and who lectures in design, and Monica Siegel, who is a translator. The bedroom overlooks a pretty stone courtyard garden in one direction and a luxurious indoor swimming pool in another.

1 The wall is lined in the original rosewood veneer □ **for wood, including cladding, see the Directory of Suppliers on pages 152–55**

2 Vertical blind in a vibrant blue, inherited from the previous owner □ **for blinds, see the Directory of Suppliers on pages 152–55**

3 Atollo table lamp (1977) by Vico Magistretti. Gives direct and diffuse light through an opaline blown Murano glass diffuser □ **www.oluce.com**

4 Bedside cabinet with drawers, built in and contemporary with the house □ **for furniture designers and makers, see the Directory of Suppliers on pages 152–55**

5 Eclisse table lamp (1966) by Vico Magistretti. Eclisse translates as eclipse and the light coming from the lamp is controlled by pulling a diffuser across the bulb opening □ **www.artemide.com**

6 Wool carpet, again, in a vibrant blue, inherited from the previous owner □ **for carpets, see the Directory of Suppliers on pages 152–55**

Luester (2003) by Ingo Maurer
□ **www.ingo-maurer.com**

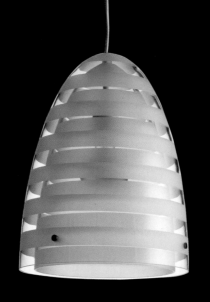

Campbell (2004) by Louise Campbell
□ **www.louis-poulsen.com**

Le Klint 173 (1969–78) by Poul Christiansen
□ **www.leklint.com**

Random Light (2002) by Monkey Boys
□ **www.moooi.com**

85 Lamps (1993) by Rodi Graumans
□ **www.droogdesign.nl**

Light Shade Shade (1999) by Jurgen Bey
□ **www.moooi.com**

Wo bist du, Edison, …? (1997) by
Ingo Maurer □ **www.ingo-maurer.com**

Le Klint 178 (1969–78) by Poul Christiansen
□ **www.leklint.com**

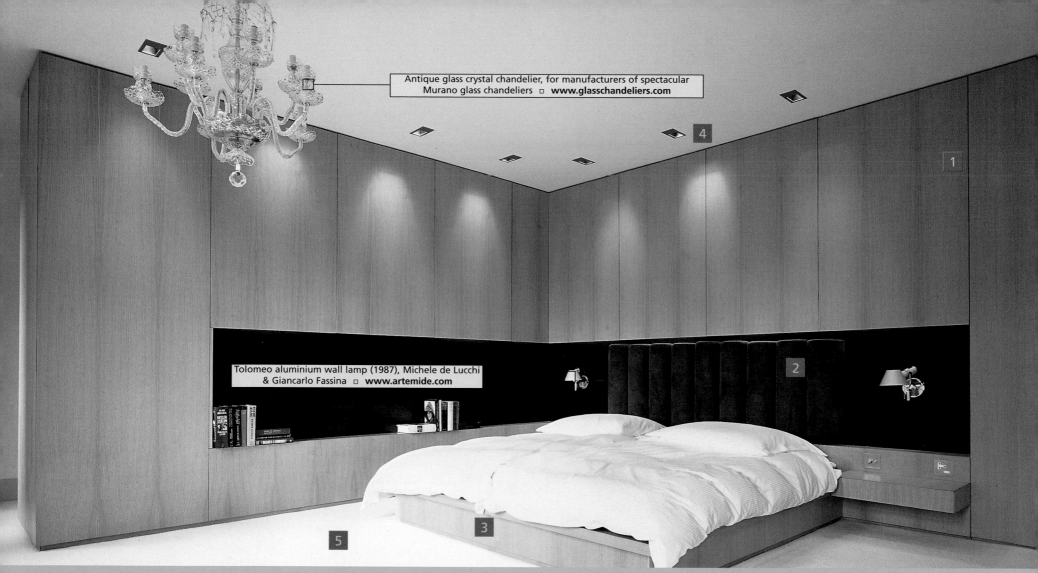

Antique glass crystal chandelier, for manufacturers of spectacular
Murano glass chandeliers □ **www.glasschandeliers.com**

Tolomeo aluminium wall lamp (1987), Michele de Lucchi
& Giancarlo Fassina □ **www.artemide.com**

Jet set chic
by Project Orange

www.projectorange.com

A retro-style bedroom has been created in the unlikely setting
of a Victorian house. The wraparound wall in panels of white-
lacquered oak veneer is a huge piece of furniture, which
incorporates a wardrobe and storage cupboards accessed from
the back. Behind here is also an en suite bathroom. The dark
horizontal band at bed level provides shelving space for books
on one wall and then turns at 90 degrees to become the
upholstered bedhead. A glittering antique crystal chandelier, a
family heirloom, provides the final glamorous flourish.

1 The wraparound wall is custom designed by the architect using oak
veneer panels, which have been finished with a translucent white
lacquer. On the outer face of the wall are wardrobes and storage space
□ **www.projectorange.com**

2 The restful line created by the low horizontal band which frames
the bed is finished in a glossy dark charcoal-coloured lacquer where it
forms a recess for books. Behind the bed, the padded headboard is
upholstered in a suede-like fabric called Glove □ **www.kvadrat.dk**

3 Bed, bespoke design by the architect □ **www.projectorange.com**

4 Recessed ceiling lights called Twin Slide, with two lamps
in each fitting for wall washing by Modular Lighting
□ **www.supermodular.com**

5 The floor covering is a neutral, stone colour wool carpet
□ **for carpets, see the Directory of Suppliers on pages 152–55**

Brera W (1992) by Achille Castiglioni
□ **www.flos.net**

Model No. WBT 77 (1977) by Benedict Tonon
□ **www.tecnolumen.de**

Io (2004) by Merete Christensen & Bo Seedorff
□ **www.louis-poulsen.com**

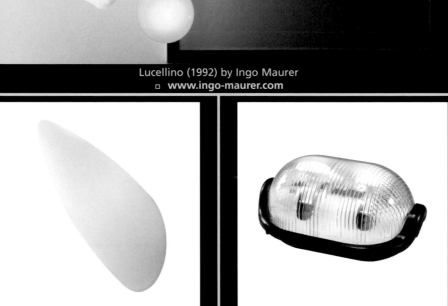

Lucellino (1992) by Ingo Maurer
□ **www.ingo-maurer.com**

Light au Lait (2004) by Fabien Dumas &
Ingo Maurer □ **www.ingo-maurer.com**

Luci Fair (1989) by Philippe Starck
□ **www.flos.net**

Noce T (1972) by Achille Castiglioni
□ **www.flos.net**

Romeo Babe wall lamp in aluminium (1998),
Philippe Starck □ **www.flos.net**

Slatted bed with wenge-coloured veneer
□ **www.boconcept.com**

Basement oasis
by John Kerr Associates

www.johnkerrassociates.com

This luxurious basement bedroom and bathroom have been created in what was, a century ago, a Jewish soup kitchen serving 6,000 people every night. The intriguing and handsome building with its red brick and terracotta façade has now been transformed into apartments. The bedroom and bathroom is part of a very spacious live/work duplex – the upstairs is bright, brisk and open where the business of the day is conducted, while below it is a darker, restful retreat furnished with handsome dark furniture and rich materials.

1 Spiral Ribbon Chandelier made by stretching cotton over a spiral frame □ **www.purves.co.uk**

2 Three-hole, wall-mounted mixer, design by Philippe Starck as part of the Axor Starck range □ **www.hansgrohe.com**

3 Cobra-Therm vertical, wall-fixed radiator in stainless steel, doubles as a heated towel rail □ **www.bisque.co.uk**

4 Plywood, counter top style of wash basin, also available by the same manufacturer in the BluToo range are basins in materials as diverse as glass, stainless steel, cedarwood and stone □ **www.minetti.de**

5 Stainless steel switches and sockets □ **www.forbesandlomax.co.uk**

6 An unusual and witty use of exterior decking material, to give this bathroom the feel of a Japanese bath house. The wood is massanduba □ **for wooden decking, see the Directory of Suppliers on pages 152–55**

7 The clever device of sinking the bath just a few centimetres below floor level, is unexpected and magically adds to the air of luxury. It is a Jazz Solo, steel inset design □ **www.duravit.com**

8 A single lever mixer tap designed by Philippe Starck as part of the Axor Starck range □ **www.hansgrohe.com**

9 Chinese seagrass floor covering. The seagrass is latex backed and also available in herringbone design □ **for natural floor coverings, see the Directory of Suppliers on pages 152–55**

Trumpet (2002) by Jorrit Kortenhorst
▫ **www.moooi.com**

Miss K (2003) by Philippe Starck
▫ **www.flos.net**

Romeo Moon T1 (1998) by Philippe Starck
▫ **www.flos.net**

Kaipo (2001) by Edward van Vliet
▫ **www.moooi.com**

One From The Heart (1989) by Ingo Maurer
▫ **www.ingo-maurer.com**

Shadows (1998) by Marcel Wanders
▫ **www.cappellini.it**

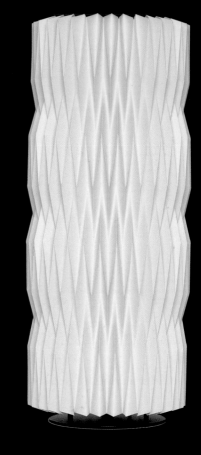

Le Klint 102 by Tove & Edv Kindt-Larsen
▫ **www.leklint.com**

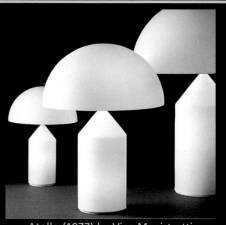

Atollo (1977) by Vico Magistretti
▫ **www.oluce.com**

Fiesta pendant lamp, Model No. PB12, in frosted white glass □ **www.radiant.co.za**

Silo table lamp, Model No. JF161, with linen shade □ **www.radiant.co.za**

Blurring the boundaries
by Marco Bezzoli, Michael Borgstrom and Adi Goren at architecture dot com
email: marco.arch@absamail.co.za

The brief for this apartment on Cape Town's Atlantic seaboard was to maximise views over the coast and create interiors that are 'earthy yet timeless'. The building's design is a pared-down palette of stainless steel, timber, stone and glass with a hint of sixties retro styling. The theme is carried through to the interiors with the use of the same materials. The interiors are primarily finished in the muted colours of the travertine tiling and off-white painted walls to dampen the sea glare. A key element of the design is the flexible open-plan interior; the feeling of spaciousness is further enhanced by the 'floating' roof structure and its band of horizontal windows, which gives a 360 degree view of the surrounding mountains, sky and sea. The bedroom and bathroom flow together with the shower behind the bed in a glass cubicle from where bathers can enjoy the sea views.

1 Bathroom wall tiled in 100 x 400mm unsealed beige Turkish travertine tiles, which were cut to size on site by the tiler □ **for tiles, see the Directory of Suppliers on pages 152–55**

2 Single-lever mixer tap in chrome from the Tower-Tech range by La Torre □ **www.latorre-spa.it**

3 Corri 1 cast marble-resin deep basin by Marble Cast □ **www.marblecast.co.za**

4 Built-in wardrobes in solid Australian jarrah wood, designed by architecture dot com □ **email: marco.arch@absamail.co.za**

5 Float 01 bed in solid Australian jarrah wood designed by architecture dot com □ **email: marco.arch@absamail.co.za**

6 Floor tiled in 600 x 600mm honed and filled, vein-cut Turkish travertine tiles □ **for tiles, see the Directory of Suppliers on pages 152–55**

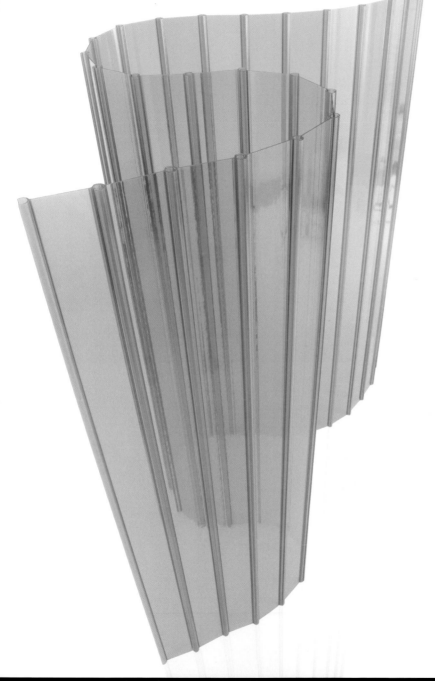

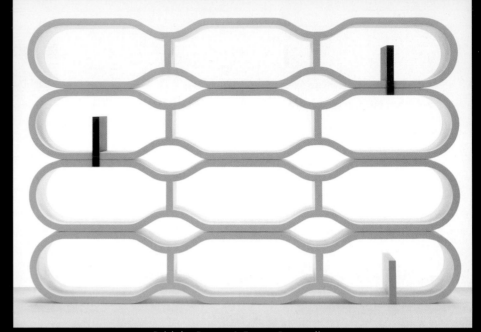

Brick by Ronan & Erwan Bouroullec
□ **www.cappellini.it**

Extendable Screen (2004) by Tom Dixon
□ **www.tomdixon.net**

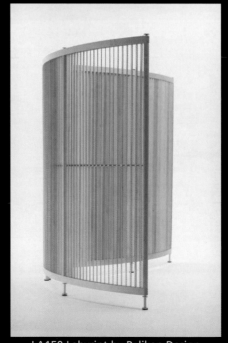

LA150 Labyrint by Pelikan Design
□ **www.fritzhansen.com**

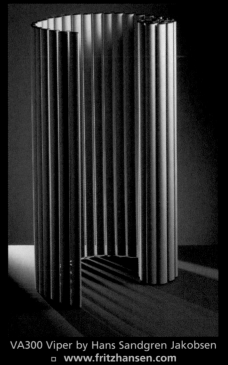

VA300 Viper by Hans Sandgren Jakobsen
□ **www.fritzhansen.com**

Screen Model No. 100 in natural lacquered pine (1933–36), Alvar Aalto □ www.artek.fi

Stool Model No. 60 in birch with white linoleum seat (1932–33), Alvar Aalto □ www.artek.fi

Rural retreat
by Knud Holscher
www.knudholscher.dk

This sleeping area forms part of an unusual open-plan summer retreat. It has been designed by internationally renowned architect and designer Knud Holscher, who has worked on projects from airports to the award-winning d line range of stainless-steel door furniture. The single storey building, used by Holscher as a holiday retreat, features a gentle barrel-vaulted roof and is wrapped round with floor-to-ceiling glass walls and doors. The only solid wall inside the building encloses the bathroom area. A contemporary take on the traditional Scandinavian holiday cabin, this structure uses a limited palette of simple materials – Danish fir is used inside and out, with sheet plywood to line the ceiling and fir for flooring. The rough-hewn square timber posts were discovered in a salvage yard.

1 Birch ply sheeting, an inexpensive, entirely practical and good-looking solution to lining the curved ceiling. Ply sheeting is widely available from all building yards and timber merchants □ **for wood, see the Directory of Suppliers on pages 152–55**

2 Extra wide Venetian blinds have been custom made to fit in each window bay □ **for blinds, see the Directory of Suppliers on pages 152–55**

3 A Knud Holscher prototype bed design, which features a platform on oversized wheels making it possible to move the bed to expand the living area. The bed also has a large padded, sliding headrest and two cantilevered shelves □ **www.knudholscher.dk**

4 Natural Danish fir floor boards given a translucent pale-grey wash, which allows the pattern of the grain to show through □ **for wood flooring, see the Directory of Suppliers on pages 152–55**

LC4 (1928) by Le Corbusier, Jeanneret & Perriand
□ **www.cassina.it**

Atlantic (2002) by Mårten Claesson, Eero Koivisto & Ola Rune
□ **www.dune-ny.com**

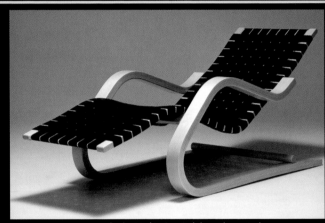

PK80 (1957) by Poul Kjærholm
□ **www.fritzhansen.com**

Lounge Chair 43 (1936–37) by Alvar Aalto
□ **www.artek.fi**

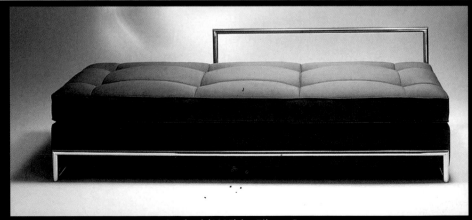

Oyster Daybed (1998) by Nigel Coates
□ **www.lloydloom.com**

Daybed (1925) by Eileen Gray
□ **www.classicon.com**

Le Klint 172 pendant lamp (1972),
Poul Christiansen □ **www.leklint.com**

1

2

3

4

5

6

7

Long Chair in birch (1935–36), Marcel Breuer
□ **www.isokonplus.com**

Best of both worlds
by Robert Dye at Robert Dye Associates
www.robertdye.com

This Regency period townhouse was in poor shape when it was brought by its current owners. The architect's brief was to refurbish and restore the place and make it fit for twentyfirst-century family life. Because the property is listed, it was important to retain and repair the period details, however contemporary design has also been integrated. After lengthy negotiations with the local planning authority, it was possible to add a modest glass extension at garden level and the designer owner has used rooms as a showcase for her designs, including wallpaper and lighting. The bedroom is an example of where the Regency backdrop has been retained, complete with picture rail and original fireplace, and then contemporary furniture and furnishings are added into the mix.

1 Wallpaper on wall and lampshade is Jocelyn Warner's oversize pattern called Oval Shimmer from the Totem range □ **www.jocelynwarner.com**

2 Oval Shimmer lampshade by Jocelyn Warner □ **www.jocelynwarner.com**

3 Print above fireplace is by Sir Charles Wheeler

4 Peep bedside table from The Conran Shop □ **www.conran.com**

5 Byron bed by Matthew Hilton. Solid American cherry or maple framed bed with veneered headboard □ **www.scp.co.uk**

6 Wire-base occasional table (1950) by Charles and Ray Eames □ **www.vitra.com**

7 A fresh look is achieved with simple white-painted floorboards. Floorpaint will look good for longer than an ordinary gloss □ **for paint, including floor paint, see the Directory of Suppliers on pages 152–55**

- a home office generates paperwork and other material, take stock of the shelving and cupboard space you need

- a desk lamp will prevent eye strain and headaches, as well as improve concentration

- a good chair is essential for day-to-day comfort and to avoid the debilitating effects of back pain. Look for ergonomic features, including adjustable padded seat and armrests, and castors

- working from home requires a substantial desk with a good size worktop – aim for an area of no less than 1.5m by 1m – set at a comfortable height

- plan shelving and cupboards for easy and immediate access to items you use every day, books or files used less often can be stored further away

- if possible, place your desk somewhere near a window; views and natural sunlight can be uplifting

Growing numbers of people are giving up commuting, canteens and office gossip to work from home, whilst those in regular employment are spending more and more time working from home. To ensure a productive and enjoyable experience, the home workspace has to be inviting and comfortable. Depending on the type of

used. If it is in a house, the bedroom/workroom is likely to be on an upper floor and therefore blessed with good natural light, and has the bonus of being separated from general family noise and disturbance. Where space is at a premium think about setting up a desk in a regularly used bedroom where it will be quiet during the

WORK SPACES

work, the space doesn't have to be enormous, but if you take your work seriously it pays to ensure the office is well designed. For most people the minimum requirement will be a desk and chair with shelving and storage. The classic home office location is the guest bedroom, which makes excellent use of a room that is otherwise under-

day. It might be worth considering an attic conversion or extension to gain valuable extra space. The desk and chair should be chosen with care – a large worksurface is ideal and an office style chair with ergonomic features will ensure that you avoid the perils and pains of back injury caused by sitting on inappropriate chairs.

Model No. S285 (1930–31) by Marcel Breuer
□ **www.thonet.de**

Model No. 2629, Radice (2001) by Roberto Barbieri
□ **www.zanotta.it**

Office System by System 180
□ **www.system180.de**

Model No. 465, Helsinki (1995) by
Caronni Bonanomi □ **www.desalto.it**

Model No. 2725, Comacina (1930) by Piero Bottoni
□ **www.zanotta.it**

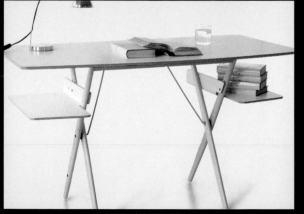

Scrittarello (1997) by Achille Castiglioni
□ **www.depadova.it**

Loop Desk (1999) by Edward Barber & Jay Osgerby
□ **www.cappellini.it**

Nomos (1989) by Foster & Partners
□ **www.tecnospa.com**

Soft Pad ea 217–219 in black leather (1969),
Charles & Ray Eames □ www.vitra.com

Burdick Group modular office system (1980),
Bruce Burdick □ www.hermanmiller.com

Zen simplicity
by Ou Baholyodhin Studio
www.ou-b.com

A home office in the famous 1930s London apartment block, Highpoint, owned by the designer Ou Baholyodhin. This room, part of a penthouse apartment, has remained largely unchanged since the apartments were designed and built by Berthold Lubetkin between 1935–38. It is a calm and uncluttered office space furnished with pieces of iconic furniture – the Eames-design Soft Pad chair is a widely acknowledged classic, the desk is by Bruce Burdick and forms part of the modular system called the Burdick Group. This is a modular system built around an interchangeable kit of parts, connected by aluminium beams and brackets, to support worksurfaces, equipment and storage elements.

1 An unusual almost sculptural shelving design believed to have been designed by the apartment's original architect, Berthold Lubetkin □ **for office furniture, including shelving, see the Directory of Suppliers on pages 152–55**

2 An intriguing wall constructed from huge slices of Norwegian fir. The intriguing texture of this wood has maximum impact when seen in such a controlled Modernist setting □ **www.nordictimber.org**

3 Earth-coloured quarry tiles, a standard product available from all good tile retailers. The contrasting white grout picks out the grid pattern □ **for stone flooring, see the Directory of Suppliers on pages 152–55**

Byrne (2000) by Eero Koivisto
□ www.david.se

Soft Pad (1969) by Charles & Ray Eames
□ www.hermanmiller.com

Model No. 3271, Oxford (1965) by
Arne Jacobsen □ www.fritzhansen.com

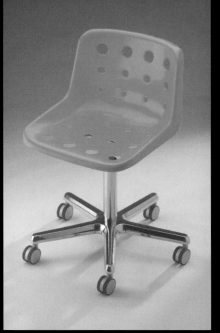

Polo Chair (1973) by Robin Day
□ www.loftonline.net

Model No. 3117, Series 7 (1955) by
Arne Jacobsen □ www.fritzhansen.com

Model No. e1, White Strip Chair by
Carlo Colombo □ www.poliform.it

Model No. 2290, Cassia (1974) by De Pas,
D'Urbino & Lomazzi □ www.zanotta.it

Aeron (1992) by Don Chadwick &
Bill Stumpf □ www.hermanmiller.com

Model No. 5263, Flow (2000) by
Burkhardt Vogtherr □ www.fritzhansen.com

Tizio desk lamp (1972), Richard Sapper
□ www.artemide.com

Kevi office chair (1974), Jørgen Rasmussen
□ www.fritzhansen.com

The pleasures of high office
by Grut Partnership &
Toh Shimazaki Architecture
email: lg@dial.pipex.com □ www.t-sa.co.uk

Raised up on the first floor of this family house, the workspace occupies pride of place at the south-facing rear of the building with views across the local park. A small extension has provided the room with a glassy roof and full-height doors which lead to the sunny terrace. One of the owners is an architect, and works at home full time, the other is an engineer, working at home some of the time. Because they spend so much of their working lives here, a good quality space was essential. In addition to a comfortable working environment, a generous sized work surface and well-ordered storage space is a must.

1 Tolomeo aluminium wall lamp (1987) by Michele de Lucchi and Giancarlo Fassina □ www.artemide.com

2 606 Universal Shelving System (1960) by Dieter Rams. A timeless, strong, handsome modular system, which along with shelving, comprises filing drawers, cupboards and worktops. The company describes its product as 'Meccano for grown ups' □ www.vitsoe.com

3 Tall, slim wall-fixed radiators. The colour was specially requested by the client □ www.hudevad.com

4 An elongated D-shaped table with ash top finished in pale grey linoleum, customised by the architect, Ann Grut. Circular and rectangular tables in birch are produced by Artek □ www.artek.fi

5 Flooring is a grey wool carpet □ for carpet, see the Directory of Suppliers on pages 152–55

6 Wastepaper bin in metal mesh □ www.ikea.com

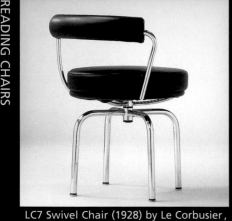

LC7 Swivel Chair (1928) by Le Corbusier,
Jeanneret & Perriand □ **www.cassina.it**

Comet by Team Johanson
□ **www.johansondesign.se**

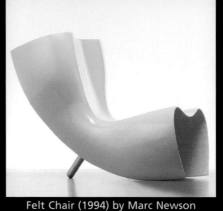

Felt Chair (1994) by Marc Newson
□ **www.cappellini.it**

Sax Mini (2004) by Terence Woodgate
□ **www.scp.co.uk**

Spanish Chair (1958) by Børge Mogensen
□ **www.fredericia.com**

Revolt (1953) by Friso Kramer
□ **www.ahrend.com**

Thinking Man's Chair (1987) by
Jasper Morrison □ **www.cappellini.it**

Model No. CH25 (1950) by Hans J. Wegner
□ **www.carlhansen.com**

LCP (Low Chair Plastic) (1996) by
Mårten van Severen □ **www.kartell.it**

Hi-Pad (1999) by Jasper Morrison
□ **www.cappellini.it**

Model No. D80 (1982) by Axel Bruchhäuser after Jean Prouvé
□ **www.tecta.de**

DCM (1946), Charles & Ray Eames from Herman Miller, also available □ **www.vitra.com**

Fibreglass Chair (1948–50), Charles & Ray Eames, from Herman Miller, reissued as Plastic Chair □ **www.vitra.com**

Library of the future
by Francine Houben at Mecanoo
www.mecanoo.com

With its far-reaching canal views, this top-floor library is a place for quiet contemplation and research. The new home sits at the end of a row of nineteenth-century houses and is planned with living space on the upper ground floor, and bedrooms and the library above. It is a house without halls and corridors and is designed with all living areas as a sequence of continuous flowing space. As this picture shows, the upper library level is linked visually to the lower living room by the use of a void by the open staircase. The threshold to the library is marked subtly in the change of flooring. The house combines stone, concrete, glass, steel and wood, solid and soft, simple and precious, in a complete composition.

1 Abstracta shelving system, designed in the 1970s by Danish architect Poul Cadovius. Abstracta is a space frame and store fixture system noted for its stability and versatility □ **www.abstracta.com**

2 Afzelia wood flooring. An extremely hardwearing African-grown wood, which possesses the durability of teak, the hardness of oak and the look of iroko □ **for wood flooring, see the Directory of Suppliers on pages 152–55**

3 Zebra pattern rug. For designer collections see □ **www.designercarpets.com**

Componibili (1967–69) by Anna Castelli Ferrieri
□ **www.kartell.it**

Kitos Modular Office System by USM
□ **www.usm.com**

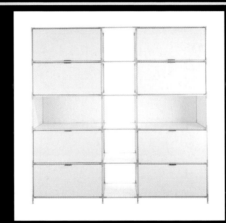

Model No. 740/50, Soho (2001–02) by
Emaf Progetti □ **www.zanotta.it**

Roller I, II, III by Marco Zanuso Jr.
□ **www.driade.com**

Plan (1999) by Jasper Morrison
□ **www.cappellini.it**

Mobil (1994) by Antonio Citterio & Glen Oliver Löw
□ **www.kartell.it**

Hard-working space

by Rainer Spehl

www.rainerspehl.com

Plenty of storage space and easy access to files, reference and papers, formed the brief for this home office design. The owner works in marketing and needed to have rapid access to information while sitting at the desk. The designer Rainer Spehl is first and foremost a furniture designer, and for his interior projects, including this office, he creates installations like large pieces of furniture. One of his trademarks is to reuse existing materials and incorporate them in his furniture. A warm-coloured backdrop for the desk was formed with sheet oak veneer, the desk top is built in, also using oak. The shelves above were made with off-the-peg brackets and MDF shelving painted olive green – a nosing at the front of the shelf hides the brackets. A bespoke-designed drawer cabinet on wheels was made to fit under the desk top. The closed cupboard wall, provides storage space for items less frequently in use.

1 A wall of tall cupboards provides capacious storage space for filing and paperwork associated with the client's job. It is used for items needed regularly but not daily. Long steel handles, add a touch of elegance. Long cabinet handles in a number of designs and made in satin stainless steel are available from various manufacturers, including d line □ **www.dline.com** □ FSB □ **www.fsb.de** □ and Allgood plc □ **www.allgood.co.uk**

2 Simple shelving kit from a regular hardware store. The planks of olive-green-painted MDF rest on standard wall brackets. A nosing has been fixed to the front of the shelves to obscure the brackets □ **for office furniture, including shelving, see the Directory of Suppliers on pages 152–55**

3 Tizio desk lamp (1972) by Richard Sapper. This lamp is the epitome of matt-black cool from the 1970s, a beautifully balanced, elegant desk lamp also available as a floor lamp □ **www.artemide.com**

4 Pine board flooring, which has been given a matt lacquer finish □ **for wood flooring, see the Directory of Suppliers on pages 152–55**

.04 office chair with flexible polyurethane foam shell, Mårten van Severen □ **www.vitra.com**

Bespoke desk and drawer unit, Rainer Spehl □ **www.rainerspehl.com**

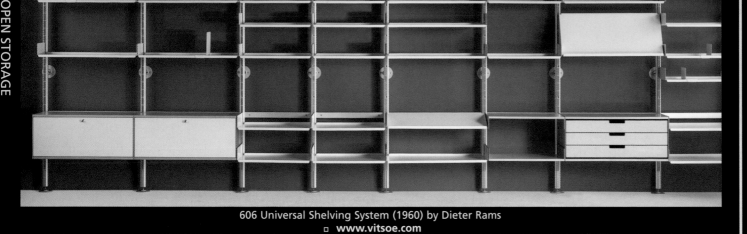

606 Universal Shelving System (1960) by Dieter Rams
□ **www.vitsoe.com**

Bookworm (1994) by Ron Arad
□ **www.kartell.it**

Model No. 731, Ulm (1996–98) by
Enzo Mari □ **www.zanotta.it**

Aliante by Giulio Cappellini &
Rodolfo Dordoni □ **www.cappellini.it**

Office System by System 180
□ **www.system180.de**

Nonus (2002) by Borre & Nygaard
□ **www.nordictrend.com**

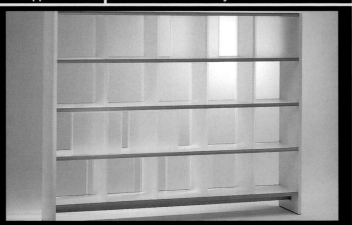

Model No. 346, Raster (2001) by Jorge Pensi
□ **www.cassina.it**

Model No. 114 Nuvola Rossa (1977) by
Vico Magistretti □ **www.cassina.it**

Speaking volumes

by Augustin + Frank Architekten

www.augustinundfrank.de

This elegant workroom with a view was created in the new-build, contemporary home designed for an antiquarian bookseller. One of the main requirements for the office was plenty of shelving to house the massive collection of books. The house was built incorporating sturdy concrete to withstand the tremendous weight of books. The vast window was constructed to introduce plenty of natural light and give fantastic, uninterrupted views over the wooded garden.

1 Lighting raft suspended over the desk to ensure good-quality light for working. It is impossible to overestimate the important of good lighting while at work, it prevents eye strain and headaches and aids concentration. Many companies produce specialist office lighting including Light Corporation ▫ **www.lightcorp.com** ▫ Erco ▫ **www.erco.com** ▫ and Louis Poulsen ▫ **www.louis-poulsen.com**

2 Modular shelving system to provide maximum storage space, and can be extended when more space is required. Low-level units in the same black-stained wood complement the bookcases. For smart contemporary systems, see Aviolux and Archi from Cappellini ▫ **www.cappellini.it** ▫ Spatio Office by Antonio Citterio and Glen Oliver Löw ▫ **www.vitra.com** ▫ and the rigorous Oikos (1998) and Kaos (1986) systems by Antonia Astori ▫ **www.driade.com**

3 A blond wood table makes a simple desk with generous size work surface. For great classic office furniture see the Knoll office systems and Knoll Studio ranges ▫ **www.knollint.com**

4 A spectacular feature of the house is this wall of glass. It was bespoke made by Gretsch-Unitas ▫ **www.g-u.de**

5 An industrial quality oak parquet, the type of hardwearing material you might find in a car showroom or shop ▫ **for wood flooring, see the Directory of Suppliers on pages 152–55**

Archimoon Tech (1998) by Philippe Starck
□ **www.flos.net**

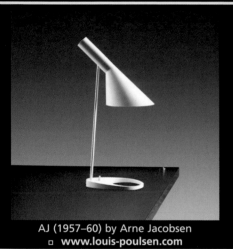

AJ (1957–60) by Arne Jacobsen
□ **www.louis-poulsen.com**

Table Lamp BS712 (1969) by Ben af Schulten
□ **www.artek.fi**

Arà (1988) by Philippe Starck
□ **www.flos.net**

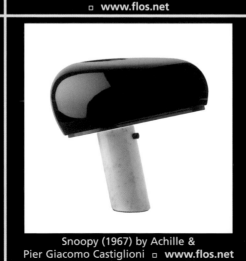

Snoopy (1967) by Achille &
Pier Giacomo Castiglioni □ **www.flos.net**

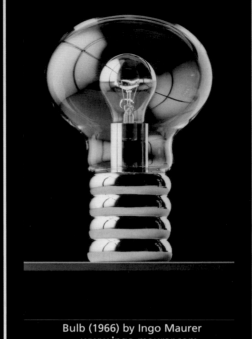

Bulb (1966) by Ingo Maurer
□ **www.ingo-maurer.com**

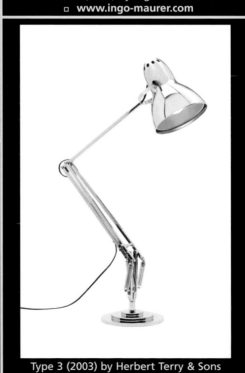

Type 3 (2003) by Herbert Terry & Sons
□ **www.anglepoise.com**

RHa (1981–84) by Dieter Rams &
Andreas Hackbarth □ **www.tecnolumen.de**

606 Universal Shelving System (1960),
Dieter Rams ▫ **www.vitsoe.com**

Oskar lamp (1998), Ingo Maurer
▫ **www.ingo-maurer.com**

High Frame chair in aluminium,
Alberto Meda ▫ **www.aliasdesign.it**

Shelf life
by Design Service at Vitsoe

www.vitsoe.com

The refurbishment of this 1960's home included opening up the entire ground floor by removing the entrance hall and its eight doors leading to various parts of the living space. A new work area was designed to fit in the previously unused space under the original stairs. On the other side of this wall is the kitchen. The classic Vitsoe 606 Universal Shelving System was used to construct the office area, part of it is wall fixed

and part is fixed between floor and ceiling where it extends beyond the end of the wall towards the dining area. A comprehensive modular system, it is constructed in aluminium, steel, wood and laminate. The wall comprises shelving, a three-drawer cabinet, three one-drawer cabinets and a small integrated laminate table. At the far end, the reverse side of the system is used for storing cutlery, linen and glasses. The use of wide-board oak flooring throughout visually ties the spaces together. For continuity, an Alberto Meda-designed High Frame chair is used at the desk as well as at the table for a dining chair.

1 The original 1960's stairs have been refurbished and the centre part of the tread wrapped in leather ▫ **for furnishings fabrics and textiles, including leather, see the Directory of Suppliers on pages 152–55**

2 Costanza pendant lamp (1985) by Paolo Rizzatto. Also available as a floor, table and wall lamp with a square natural aluminium, black or iron grey stand. The silk-screen printed polycarbonate shade is available in a range of colours ▫ **www.luceplan.com**

3 Vitsoe dining table, which is no longer in production and is now a collector's item ▫ **for vintage furniture, see the Directory of Suppliers on pages 152–55**

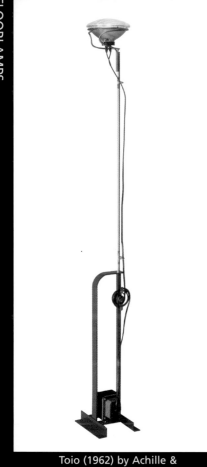

Toio (1962) by Achille &
Pier Giacomo Castiglioni □ **www.flos.net**

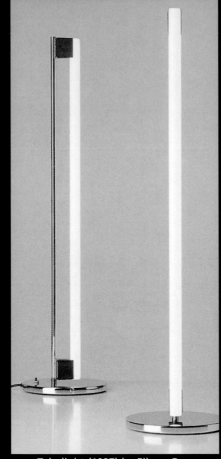

Tubelight (1927) by Eileen Gray
□ **www.classicon.com**

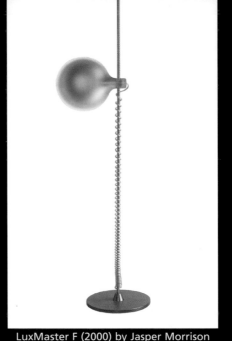

LuxMaster F (2000) by Jasper Morrison
□ **www.flos.net**

Parentesi (1970) by Achille Castiglioni &
Pio Manzu □ **www.flos.net**

Prototype (2002) by Ingo Maurer & Bernhard Dessecker
□ **www.ingo-maurer.com**

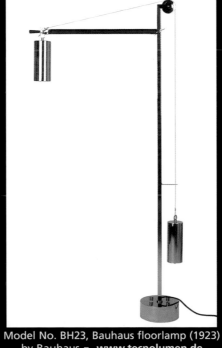

Model No. BH23, Bauhaus floorlamp (1923)
by Bauhaus □ **www.tecnolumen.de**

Trapeze low-voltage track lighting system
□ **www.mr-resistor.co.uk**

Soft Pad ea 217–219 in black leather (1969),
Charles & Ray Eames □ **www.vitra.com**

Fertile imagination
by Mary Manatiy at
Marston Manatiy Design
www.marstonmanatiydesign.com

As part of the refurbishment of an elegant
nineteenth-century London riverside apartment,
the former Japanese-style conservatory has been
cleverly converted for use as a home office. It
sits on the second floor of the building and has
magnificent views. To help protect the interior
from overheating in full sunlight, floor-to-ceiling
blinds have been fitted round the whole interior.
To maximise enjoyment of, and to reflect, the
cityscape, the natural light and constantly
moving river, the refurbishment of the home has
included a liberal use of clear and coloured glass
and mirrors.

1 An antique triple-stem globe lamp from the 1960s,
a secondhand find. The lamp is reminiscent of the great
Arco of 1962 by Achille and Pier Giacomo Castiglioni,
for Flos □ **www.flos.net**

2 Cedar floral wood slat Venetian blinds
□ **for blinds, see the Directory of Suppliers on
pages 152–55**

3 Thirties-style steel desk by Müller, part of the Classic
Line range of units □ **www.mueller-moebel.com**

4 American oak, engineered planks with oiled finish
□ **for wood flooring, see the Directory of Suppliers on
pages 152–55**

5 Tan leather storage box
□ **www.theholdingcompany.co.uk**

Model. No. T0521, Butterfly Stool (1956) by
Sori Yanagi □ **www.tendo-mokko.co.jp**

Model No. EJ 144 by Anne Mette Jensen &
Morten Ernst □ **www.erik-joergensen.com**

Jakkara by Durat
□ **www.durat.com**

Corks (2002) by Jasper Morrison
□ **www.moooi.com**

La Bohème (2001) by Philippe Starck
□ **www.kartell.it**

Time-Life Stool (1960) by Charles &
Ray Eames □ **www.vitra.com**

PK33 (1959) by Poul Kjærholm
□ **www.fritzhansen.com**

18 inch polished stool (2002) by
Philippe Starck □ **www.emeco.net**

Model No. 220, Mezzadro (1957) by
Achille Castiglioni □ **www.zanotta.it**

Table Lamp BS712 (1969),
Ben af Schulten □ www.artek.fi

Stool Model No. 60 in birch with red linoleum seat
(1932–33), Alvar Aalto □ www.artek.fi

Rest, work and play
by Haroma Partners
www.haromapartners.fi

With an enviable position on the banks of a river, this former brick-built school building has now been converted into simple, loft-style apartments. A double-height space at the window end of the rectangular apartment is used for the dining and sitting areas. Towards the back, is a mezzanine floor, underneath which is the kitchen and bathroom, while above is this open-plan bedroom and home office. A unifying factor in this simple interior is the choice of furniture all from the same family made in birch wood and designed by Finnish architect Alvar Aalto (1898–1976) who set up his own company, Artek, to manufacturer his designs.

1 Zebra pattern rug. For designer collections see □ **www.designercarpets.com**

2 A daybed called 710 was designed by Alvar Aalto and remains in production. Meanwhile another of his bed designs based on a steel tube frame is made by Wohnbedarf Basel □ **www.wohnbedarf.com**

3 Table 80A (1933–35) by Alvar Aalto. A birch wood table, which doubles as a desk, with red linoleum surface □ **www.artek.fi**

4 Chair 611 (1929–30) by Alvar Aalto. A stackable, birch wood chair with black webbing upholstery. Also available with leather seating □ **www.artek.fi**

5 Pedestal 297 (1929–30) by Alvar Aalto. A birch made stack of five shallow drawers which can rest on a plinth, as shown here, or be fitted with castors □ **www.artek.fi**

- to make a small outside space appear larger, add a sculpture or water feature to the furthest wall to draw the eye through the space; when illuminated, it will look particularly impressive at night

- a small shed or storage box is always useful for stowing away any extra cushions, rugs, candles, deck chairs and a few garden tools

- mirrors fixed to walls create the illusion of extra space

- garden lighting can be magical – use spotlights to illuminate trees or chains of fairy lights around a dining area; keep light levels low to avoid annoying neighbours

- a table and chairs are essential for making a social space – opt for the luxury of teak or practicality of materials like aluminium which can be left outside

- an outdoor sound system is a real luxury

Gardens and outdoor spaces not only look different from a few years ago, they are also being used in other ways. Traditional lawns with herbaceous borders have given way to low-maintenance gardens. You don't need a huge space to enjoy being outside, even the smallest balcony or terrace can be colonised with a table, chairs and potted plants. The garden has become an extension of the interior and, in many homes, the main living room is now facing the garden where blurring the boundaries between inside and out is achieved with sliding and folding doors. An outdoor room should be used as often as possible; it is a place to entertain family and friends, and to let your imagination run wild, be frivolous or outrageous in your designs. Just as you would decorate a room, think about flooring materials and colour schemes, the style of furniture and lighting. There is also the opportunity to add extra interest perhaps with a water feature, expand the sense of space with mirrors, or add a sculpture in the distance to draw the eye through the space. To help achieve the desired effect designers and manufacturers are producing ranges of beautiful outdoor furniture, interesting decking and paving materials, sophisticated barbecues and ovens, café style heaters and excellent outdoor lighting.

OUTDOOR SPACES

Arne Jacobsen Seat by Arne Jacobsen
□ **www.listerteak.com**

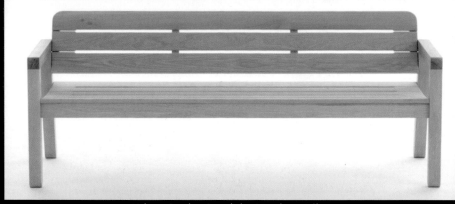

Urban Garden Bench by Matthew Hilton
□ **www.scp.co.uk**

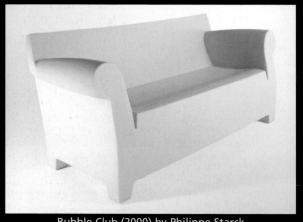

Bubble Club (2000) by Philippe Starck
□ **www.kartell.it**

Phantom (2004) by Peter Emrys-Roberts
□ **www.driade.com**

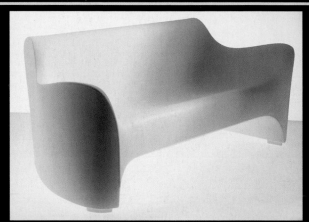

Tokyo-Pop (2002) by Tokujin Yoshioka
□ **www.kartell.it**

Model No. 980, Camilla (1984) by
Castiglioni & Pozzi □ **www.zanotta.it**

Haven by Barlow Tyrie
□ **www.barlowtyrie.com**

Court Seat by Christian Gaze
□ **www.gazeburvill.com**

No Limit table with zinc-covered extending end for planters, Kerstin Olby □ **www.olbydesign.se**

Element aluminium wall lights, Kina Strandberg & Marie Lundgren □ **www.smakdesign.se**

String lounger in pine, Kerstin Olby □ **www.olbydesign.se**

Sun, moon and stars
Nina Thalinson at Lust & Fägring
www.lustochfagring.se

Even the smallest garden becomes a beautiful and welcoming place with ingenious lighting and appealing materials. This urban design is conceived as an extension to the house and as a place to enjoy the sun as well as the stars in the night-time sky. The pergola makes a framework for the dining space furnished with table and stools. The net of tiny lights guarantees a romantic starry evening even when it is cloudy.

1 The pergola is constructed from steel beams covered with a net studded with tiny low-voltage bulbs. The frame acts a climbing support for Humulus Japonicus, an ornamental vine also known as the Japanese hop □ **for lighting, see the Directory of Suppliers on pages 152–55**

2 The waterfall feature is made of glass bricks set in a steel frame. A pump ensures steady and slow trickles of water down the face of the glass bricks. A sheet of aluminium foil has been fixed to the wall behind the bricks to act as a reflector for the light from a pair of lamps, also fixed behind the bricks. There is a 500mm gap between wall and glass bricks □ **www.lustochfagring.se**

3 Plant pots made of sand-cast recycled aluminium from Byarums Bruk □ **www.byarumsbruk.se**

4 Pall Lilla Li stools with rope seats by Kerstin Olby □ **www.olbydesign.se**

5 Big concrete pots, with glass staves for climbing plants designed by Nina Thalinson and Eva Paradis, handmade at the Paradis Workshop □ **www.paradisverstaden.se**

6 Grey paving bricks, framed by concrete paving of larger pinkish bricks with a flower relief pattern, designed by Cissa Sundling □ **www.lustochfagring.se**

Model No. C4 A-D, Nesting Tables (1925–26)
by Marcel Breuer □ **www.tecta.de**

Broadway Round Table by Lister Teak
□ **www.listerteak.com**

FOG Table (1999) by Frank O. Gehry
□ **www.knoll.com**

MR Side Table (1927–29) by Ludwig
Mies van der Rohe □ **www.knoll.com**

Equinox by Barlow Tyrie
□ **www.barlowtyrie.com**

Windsor by Barlow Tyrie
□ **www.barlowtyrie.com**

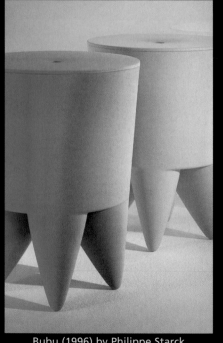

Bubu (1996) by Philippe Starck
□ **www.xo-design.com**

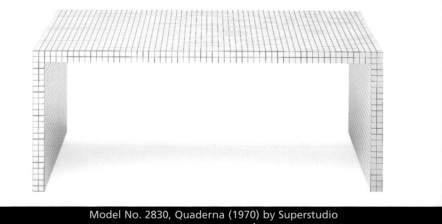

Model No. 2830, Quaderna (1970) by Superstudio
□ **www.zanotta.it**

Dining table with zinc top, Stephen Woodhams
□ **www.woodhams.co.uk**

Dining out in the urban jungle
Stephen Woodhams at Woodhams
www.woodhams.co.uk

Rising from the urban jungle is this African-themed roof terrace that sits on the eighteenth floor and has spectacular citywide views. The design is conceived as an extension of the apartment interior below, which incorporates many of the same materials, colours and textures. The unusual herringbone pattern terrace might usually be built in brick, but here has been laid like a parquet flooring and is made using three types of wood, iroko being prominent. The handsome dining table is completed with a pair of throne-like chairs and beside this is a small sculpture garden where the lead sculptures are reminiscent of the shapes of spears and shields. Views are made possible even when seated, through the addition of glass panel balustrading.

1 A mixture of plants has been chosen, grasses include *Carex bucchanii* mixed with *Astelia chathamica* 'Silver Spear' and bamboo □ **www.woodhams.co.uk**

2 Zinc sculptures in shapes reminiscent of spears and shields by Sean Brosnan □ **www.woodhams.co.uk**

3 Planters add their own sculptural quality to the space, and are available in a wide range of materials □ **for garden furniture, see the Directory of Suppliers on pages 152–55**

4 Throne chairs in oak with brushed stainless steel-clad backs, bespoke design by Stephen Woodhams □ **www.woodhams.co.uk**

5 A herringbone pattern floor made in timber, predominantly iroko □ **for wooden decking, see the Directory of Suppliers on pages 152–55**

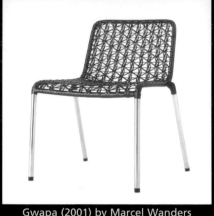

Gwapa (2001) by Marcel Wanders
□ **www.moooi.com**

Mauna-Kea (1993) by Vico Magistretti
□ **www.kartell.it**

Model No. 2260, Celestina (1978) by
Marco Zanuso □ **www.zanotta.it**

Kingsley Small Folding Chair by
Lister Teak □ **www.listerteak.com**

Model No. 2068, Mirandolina (1992) by
Pietro Arosio □ **www.zanotta.it**

Model No. D 4, Foldable Armchair (1927)
by Marcel Breuer □ **www.tecta.de**

Model No. S40F (1998) by Thonet after
Mart Stam □ **www.thonet.de**

Model No. 2076, Zilli (2002) by
Roberto Barbieri □ **www.zanotta.it**

Model No. KS200, Ice (2003) by
Kasper Salto □ **www.fritzhansen.com**

Model No. 2120, April (1964) by
Gae Aulenti □ **www.zanotta.it**

Less work and more play

Karena Batstone at Karena Batstone
Design & Helen Tindale at Reversed Out

www.karenabatstone.com ▫

www.reversedout.com

The owners of this long town garden wanted a
space which was easy to maintain, a place for
entertaining and enjoying food outside and an
safe area for their child to play. The designers
began by raising the level of the garden – it had
been accessed from the basement level, but
raising it made it much more easily accessed from
the ground floor. There are now steps up from
the basement. A dining area was created using
stone paving – this was pushed away from the
house, to encourage better use of the garden. It
also means that grown ups can keep a close
watch on playing children. A 'secret' play area has
been created at the far end of the garden behind
the large wall of opal acrylic sheeting.

1 Opal coloured acrylic sheet ▫ **for plastics, see the
Directory of Suppliers on pages 152–55**

2 Stainless-steel planters made by specialist
metalworker ▫ **www.elitemetalcraft.co.uk**

3 Stone paving supplied by the client. It is vital to select
a stone which is appropriate for the location. Where
frost is likely to occur materials including York Stone and
Sandstone are a good idea. Ceramic tiles may also be
used as well as slate and marble. Check with your
supplier ▫ **for stone paving, see the Directory of
Suppliers on pages 152–55**

4 Lighting has been carefully located around the
garden and includes uplighters to illuminate the pretty
silver birch trees ▫ **for suppliers of lighting see page
152 of the Directory**

5 Slate chippings are used to create the path
and boundary between dining area and grass
▫ **for stone paving, see the Directory of Suppliers on
pages 152–55**

Slick-Slick stackable chair in polypropylene (1999),
Philippe Starck ▫ **www.xo-design.com**

Thali table in anodised aluminium with slatted top,
Miki Astori ▫ **www.driade.com**

Safari Chair (1933) by Kaare Klint
□ **www.rudrasmussen.dk**

Lord Yo (1994) by Philippe Starck
□ **www.driade.com**

Haven Armchair with Ottoman by Barlow Tyrie
□ **www.barlowtyrie**

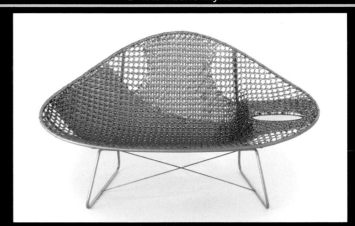

Flower Chair (2001) by Marcel Wanders
□ **www.moooi.com**

Dalai Daybed by Hyacinth
□ **www.hyacinth-design.com**

Lovenet (2002) by Ross Lovegrove
□ **www.moooi.com**

KAAT Armchair by Wilfried Hendriks &
Steven Stals □ **www.listerteak.com**

Nemo (2003) by Jane Dillon & Tom Grieves
□ **www.lloydloom.com**

Throw-away (1965) by Willie Landels
□ **www.zanotta.it**

Upholstered armchair, for similar see Haven from Barlow Tyrie □ www.barlowtyrie.com

The pleasure garden
by Candy and Candy
www.candyandcandy.com

With growing numbers of city and town dwellers wanting to enjoy some outside space, there has been a tremendous growth in roof gardens. Even the very smallest of spaces can be transformed into a private terrace. Here among the chimneys pots, a tiny terrace has been given an exotic Middle Eastern theme with the timber built daybed and a pair of extremely comfortable upholstered armchairs. A mirror is cleverly positioned to introduce reflections, which enhance the sense of space in this compact area. A sculpture and candle sticks are decorative accessories. The slow-growing hedge provides a natural screen from the homes on the opposite side of the road.

1 Bespoke simple daybed by Candy and Candy, which fits into the niche beside the chimney pots. It has been designed so that the canvas top is easily removed and stowed away with the cushions to protect them from the weather □ **www.candyandcandy.com**

2 Privacy is secured with this slow-growing hedge, which provides a natural screen from the homes opposite □ **for garden plants, see the Directory of Suppliers on pages 152–55**

3 Cedar wood decking, which is tough and durable. The grooved surface helps to prevent slipping □ **for wooden decking, see the Directory of Suppliers on pages 152–55**

4 Floor recessed lights add an extra dimension to this terrace, making it welcoming at night □ **for lighting, see the Directory of Suppliers on pages 152–55**

Natal Chaise Longue by Wim Segers
□ **www.tribu.be**

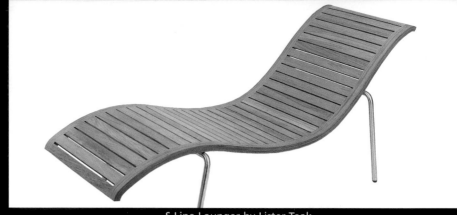

S Line Lounger by Lister Teak
□ **www.listerteak.com**

PK24 (1965) by Poul Kjærholm
□ **www.fritzhansen.com**

Seagull Lounger by Lister Teak
□ **www.listerteak.com**

Bowline Lounger (2004) by Gaze Burvill
□ **www.gazeburvill.com**

Model No. 930, Soft (1999) by Werner Aisslinger
□ **www.zanotta.it**

Lounger Model No. 5090, Lister Teak
□ www.listerteak.com

Town garden
by The Plant Room
www.plantroom.co.uk

The owners of this town garden wanted a space for resting and entertaining which would involve minimal maintenance. The design is cleverly based on the diagonal across the long, but narrow garden, which makes an eyecatching layout and enhances the sense of space. Decking is set at different levels to landscape the area and break it into distinct spaces for sunbathing or dining. Planting, in ground level and raised beds, is designed to require as little maintenance as possible and plants are set in small beds mulched with white cockle shells which reflect the light and add textural interest. There is also an inbuilt irrigation system and wiring for outdoor lighting

1 Bespoke triangular shed designed by The Plant Room to fit into this corner of the garden. It provides valuable storage space for cushions, outdoor lights and candles, a minimal number of garden tools and a brush for sweeping the decking □ **www.plantroom.co.uk**

2 An extremely clever and space-efficient way of achieving outdoor seating, this uses part of the blue-painted, blockwork retaining wall as an L-shaped seat to wrap round a large bespoke limestone-topped table. Although this is a small area, it can comfortably seat up to ten people □ **www.plantroom.co.uk**

3 A contemporary pergola built using timber posts and regular copper piping from a builder's merchant. It provides the structure for this ancient Italian vine to clamber over □ **www.plantroom.co.uk**

4 To keep the budget down on this particular project softwood decking was chosen. It is set at different levels to landscape the area and break it into distinct spaces. Another way of subtly separating the areas has been to lay the boards on each level at 90 degrees to the adjoining deck. Decking is widely available; all garden designers and good retailers will offer advice on what to choose □ **for wooden decking, see the Directory of Suppliers on pages 152–55**

Directory of suppliers

Associations and industry bodies

British Woodworking Federation
56–64 Leonard Street
London EC2A 4JX
0870 458 6939a
www.bwf.org.uk

The Concrete Centre
Riverside House
4 Meadows Business Park
Station Approach
Blackwater
Camberley
Surrey GU17 9AB
National Helpline 0700 4500 500
www.concretecentre.com

Federation of Master Builders
Gordon Fisher House
14–15 Great James Street
London WC1N 3DP
020 7242 7583
www.fmb.org.uk

Forest Stewardship Council UK
Unit D, Station Building
Llanidloes
Powys SY18 6EB
01686 413916
www.fsc-uk.info
International body that certificates sustainable timber

Royal Institute of British Architects
Client Services
66 Portland Place
London W1B 1AD
020 7580 5533
www.architecture.com

The Stone Federation of Great Britain
Channel Business Centre
Ingles Manor
Castle Hill Avenue
Folkestone
Kent CT20 2RD
01303 856123
www.stone-federationgb.org.uk

Timber Decking Association
CIRCE Building
Wheldon Road
Castleford
West Yorkshire WF10 2JT
01977 712718
www.tda.org.uk

Timber Trade Federation
Clareville House
26/27 Oxendon Street
London SW1Y 4EL
020 7839 1891
www.ttf.co.uk

Aquariums and fish tanks

John Allan Aquariums Ltd
Eastern Industrial Estate
Eastern Way
Bury St. Edmunds
Suffolk IP32 7AB
01284 755051
www.johnallanaquariums.com

Aqualease
PO Box 330
Blackburn
Lancashire BB2 3XX
01254 278807
www.aqualease.co.uk

Aquatic Design
109 Great Portland Street
London W1W 6QG
020 7636 6388
www.aquaticdesign.co.uk

Architectural glass

Cantifix
Unit 22, Garrick Industrial Centre
Irving Way
London NW9 6AQ
020 8203 6203
www.cantifix.co.uk

J. Preedy and Sons
Lamb Works
North Road
London N7 9DP
020 7700 0377
Design and installation of glass flooring, glass panels and mirrors

Pilkington UK Ltd
Prescot Road
St Helens
Cheshire WA10 3TT
01744 692000
Huge range of decorative glass, low-emmisivity glass and other high-specification types

Schott (UK) Ltd
Drummond Road
Astonfields Industrial Estate
Stafford ST16 3EL
01785 223166
01785 223522
www.schottglass.co.uk

Solarglass
Herald Way, Binley
Coventry CV3 2ND
01203 458844
Architectural glass, including an electrically operated glass that changes from translucent to clear when a current is passed through

Architectural ironmongery

Allgood plc
297 Euston Road
London NW1 3AQ
020 7387 9951
www.allgood.co.uk
Also with branches in Manchester, Birmingham and Glasgow

Danico
31–35 Winchester Road
London NW3 3NR
020 7483 4477
email: sales@danico.co.uk

T.F. Sampson Ltd
Creeting Road
Stowmarket
Suffolk IP14 5BA
01449 613535

Architectural salvage

Machells & Sons Ltd
Low Mills, Guiseley
Leeds LS20 9LT
01132 505043
www.machells.com
Recycled building materials and period architectural features

LASSCO
Mark Street (off Paul Street)
London EC2A 4ER
020 7749 9944
www.lassco.co.uk
Architectural antiques, including fireplaces, stained glass, chandeliers and much more

Retrouvious
2a Ravensworth Road
London NW10 5NR
020 8960 6060
www.retrouvious.com
Architectural antiques, reclaimed materials and contemporary design

Bathroom furniture and fittings

Alternative Plans
9 Hester Road
London SW1 4AN
020 7228 6460
www.alternative-plans.co.uk
Contemporary bathrooms and kitchens

Bathrooms International
4 Pont Street
London SW1X 9EL
020 7838 7788
www.bathroomsint.com

Bathstore.com
www.bathstore.com
See website for your nearest store

C.P. Hart
Newnham Terrace
Hercules Road
London SE1 7DR
020 7902 1000 for branches
www.cphart.co.uk
Traditional and modern designs

Deep Blue
299–313 Lewisham High Street
London SE13 6NW
020 8690 3401
Cutting edge contemporary designers, including Hansgrohe

Original Bathrooms
143–145 Kew Road
Richmond
Surrey TW9 2PN
020 8940 7554
www.original-bathrooms.co.uk
Innovative bathroom retailer

Concrete flooring, basins and worktops

Cast Advanced Concretes
Unit 4, Rempstone Barns
Corfe Castle
Wareham
Dorset BH20 5JH
01929 480757
Concrete products for kitchens and bathrooms, including worktops, basins and furniture

Pallam Precast
187 West End Lane
West Hampstead
London NW6 2LJ
020 7328 6512
Concrete in a huge range of finishes for worktops, basins, floors, stairs and panels

Paul Davies Design
Unit 5, Parkworks
16 Park Road
Kingston-Upon-Thames
Surrey KT2 6BG
020 8541 0838
Concrete in a huge range of finishes for worktops, basins, floors, stairs and panels

Carpets and rugs

Art Rugs
01273 770877
www.artrugs.co.uk
Hand-tufted rugs in contemporary styles. Bepoke design service

Ikea

Ikea
Brent Park, 2 Drury Way
North Circular Road
London NW10 0TH
020 8208 5600
www.ikea.com
Branches nationwide

John Lewis
278–306 Oxford Street
London W1 1EX
020 7629 7711
www.johnlewis.com
Branches nationwide

Loomah Ltd
6 Sanford Lane
London N16 7LS
020 7923 0030
Handmade carpets and rugs in all colours, shapes and sizes. Bespoke design service

Roger Oates Design
1 Munro Terrace (off Riley Street)
London SW10 0DL
020 7351 2288 (and for stockists)
www.rogeroates.com
Handmade rugs in wool, linen or cotton

The Rug Company
124 Holland Park Avenue
London W11 4UE
020 7229 5148
www.therugcompany.info
Rugs from designers including Paul Smith, Marni and Matthew Williamson

Furnishing fabrics and textiles

Bute Fabrics Ltd
Barone Road
Rothesay
Isle of Bute PA20 0DP
01700 503734
www.butefabrics.com
Contemporary upholstery fabrics, projects include collaborations with designers such as Matthew Hilton, Jasper Morrison and Tom Dixon

Ian Mankin
109 Regents Park Road
London NW1 8UR
020 7722 0997
Timeless natural fabrics in utilitarian stripes, checks and plains

Kvadrat Ltd
62 Princedale Road
London W11 4NL
020 7229 9969
www.kvadrat.dk
Curtain and upholstery fabrics, from designers such as Arne Jacobsen and Ray Eames

Fires, stoves and fireplaces

Chesney's
194/202 Battersea Park Road
London SW11 4ND
020 7627 1410
www.chesneys.co.uk
Traditional and contemporary fireplaces

CVO Firevault
36 Great Titchfield Street
London W1W 8BQ
020 7580 5333
www.cvo.co.uk
Contemporary fireplaces

The Platonic Fireplace Company
Phoenix Wharf
Eel Pie Island
Twickenham
Middlesex TW1 3DY
020 8891 5904
www.platonicfireplaces.co.uk
*Manufacturer and retailer of striking
contemporary fireplaces*

Real Flame
80 New Kings Road
Parsons Green
London SW6 4LT
020 7731 2704/3056
www.realflame.co.uk
*A wide selection of beautiful modern and
traditional firegrates, with optional fitted
Real Flame gas fires*

Furniture designers and makers

Dominic Ash
www.dominicash.co.uk

John Barnard
The Design Workshop
The Granary
Trowesbridge
Norwich
Norfolk NR1 2EG
01603 623959
www.norfolk-furnituremakers.co.uk
Modern fitted and freestanding furniture

Fiske Interiors Ltd
1120 Uxbridge Road
Hayes
Middlesex UB4 8QH
020 8569 2766

Maxwell Pinborough Ltd
398–399 Mentmore Terrace
London E8 3PH
020 8525 5522
www.maxwellpinborough.com
Bespoke contemporary furniture and interiors

Furniture and home accessories

Aram Designs
110 Drury Lane
London WC2B 5SG
020 7557 7557
www.aram.co.uk

Atomic Interiors
Plumptre Square
Nottingham NG1 1JF
0115 941 5577
www.atomicinteriors.co.uk

Atrium
Centrepoint, 22–24 St Giles High Street
London WC2H 8TA
020 7379 7288
www.atriumltd.uk
Contemporary furniture and lighting

B&B Italia
250 Brompton Road
London SW3
020 7591 8111
www.bebitalia.com

The Bachelor Pad
36 St Stephen Street
Edinburgh EH3 5AL
www.thebachelorpad.org

Bo Concept
158 Tottenham Court Road
London W1 7NH
020 7388 2447
www.boconcept.com
Elegant minimal furniture and modular shelving

Capsule Furniture
126 Charles Street
Leicester LE1 1LB
0116 262 6932
Modern classic furniture and lighting

The Conran Shop
81 Fulham Road
London SW3 6RD
020 7589 7401
www.conran.com

Geoffrey Drayton
85 Hampstead Road
London NW1 2PL
020 7387 5840
www.geoffrey-drayton.co.uk
Modern classic storage and furniture

Coexistence
288 Upper Street
London N1 2TZ
0207 354 8817
www.coexistence.co.uk
Contemporary furniture and fittings

European Design Centre
77 Margaret Street
London W1W 8SY
020 7323 3233
www.edcplc.com
Contemporary furniture

Habitat
196 Tottenham Court Road
London W1T 7LG
www.habitat.net (for branches)
Good value furniture, lighting and accessories

Fritz Hansen
20–22 Rosebery Avenue
London EC1R 4SX
020 7837 2030
www.fritzhansen.com
Contemporary furniture

Heal's
196 Tottenham Court Road
London W1P 9LD
020 7636 1666
Storage, furniture, lighting and home accessories

Herman Miller
1st Floor
Maple House
149 Tottenham Court Road
London W1P 0JA
020 7388 7331
www.hermanmiller.com/uk

Ikea
Brent Park, 2 Drury Way
North Circular Road
London NW10 0TH
020 8208 5600
www.ikea.com
*Units and accessories. Excellent value for smart
Scandinavian design. Branches nationwide*

Inflate
1 Helmsley Place
London E8 3SB
020 7249 3034
www.inflate.co.uk
Innovative designers of furniture and lighting

Key London
92 Wimpole Street
London W1G 0EE
020 7499 9461
www.key-london.com
Furnishing and more

Knoll International
1 Lindsey Street
East Market
Smithfield
London EC1A 9PQ
020 7236 6655
www.knollint.com

Loft
Simpsons Field
24 Dick Street
Leeds LS10 1JF
0113 305 1515
www.loftonline.co.uk

MDF Italia
Via Morimondo 5/7
20143 Milan
Italy
00 39 0281804001 (for suppliers)
www.mdfitalia.it
Sleek Italian furniture

Nordic Interiors
130 Wigmore Street
London W1U 3SB
020 7486 0330
www.nordicinteriors.com
Contemporary furniture and furnishings

Purves & Purves
220 Tottenham Court Road
London W1T 7PZ
020 7580 8223
www.purves.co.uk

Skandium
86 Marylebone High Street
London W1U 4QS
020 7935 2077
www.skandium.com
*Quality Scandinavian furniture, lighting,
fabrics and other accessories. Also branch
in Manchester*

SCP
135–139 Curtain Road
London EC2A 3BX
020 7739 1869
www.scp.co.uk
Modern storage, furniture and lighting

System 180
Addlestone
Surrey KT15 2DF
01932 858859
www.system180.co.uk
*Award-winning modular metal construction
system for shelving and furniture*

Tangram
33/37 Jeffrey Street
Edinburgh EH1 1DH
0131 556 6551
www.tangramfurnishers.co.uk

Twentytwentyone
274 Upper Street
London N1 2UA
020 7288 1996
www.twentytwentyone.com
Furniture and lighting design classics

Viaduct Furniture
1–10 Summers Street
London EC1R 5BD
020 7278 8456
www.viaduct.co.uk
Contemporary furniture

Vitra
30 Clerkenwell Road
London EC1M 5PQ
020 7608 6200
www.vitra.com

Garden furniture and lighting

*See also listings under Furniture and
home accessories*

Cargo HomeShop
Dormer Road
Thame
Oxfordshire OX9 3HD
01844 261800
www.cargohomeshop.com
Good value garden furniture

Finn Stone
25 Cumberland Road
London N22 7TD
020 8889 3856
www.finnstone.com
*Contemporary outdoor seating, including the
Ball Chair in fibreglass and polyethylene*

Lighting for Gardens Ltd
20 Furmston Court
Icknield Way
Letchworth Garden City
Herts SG6 1UJ
01462 486777
www.lightingforgardens.com
A wide range of garden lighting solutions

Garden plants

Crocus.co.uk Ltd
Nursery Court
London Road
Windlesham
Surrey GU20 6LQ
0870 442 2798
www.crocus.co.uk
*Online garden centre for tools and plants, as
well as a design service*

Dig-it
Freepost NAT 12033
Cannock WS11 7BR
08707 54 18 22
www.dig-it.co.uk
*A wide range of contemporary garden products,
including furniture, lighting and plants*

Kitchen furniture and fittings

Allmilmo
Unit 5, Rivermead
Pipers Way
Thatcham
Berkshire RG19 4EP
01635 868181 (for stockists)
Modern kitchen designs

Almo UK
Unit 10, Hampton Farm Industrial Estate
Hampton Road
West Hanworth
Middlesex TW13 6DB
020 8898 4781 (for stockists)
www.almo.co.uk
Modern unit designs

Alternative Plans
9 Hester Road
London SW11 4AN
020 7228 6460
www.alternative-plans.co.uk
Specialists in systems by makers such as Boffi

Artichoke
Hortswood
Long Lane
Wrington
Bristol BS40 5SP
01934 863 840
www.artichoke-ltd.com
Bespoke kitchens and cabinets, all made from sustainable timber

Bulthaup
37 Wigmore Street
London W1U 1PN
020 7495 3663
www.bulthaup.com
Cutting-edge modern designs

Fulham Kitchens
19 Carnwath Road
London SW6 3HR
020 7736 6458
Designers and builders of bespoke kitchens

Miele UK
Fairacres
Marcham Road
Abingdon OX14 1TW
01235 233533 (for stockists)
www.miele.co.uk
Smart kitchens and appliances

Poggenpohl UK Ltd
Lloyds Court
681–685 Silbury Boulevard
Milton Keynes MK9 3AZ
01908 247600 (for stockists)
www.poggenpohl.de
Contemporary German kitchen designs

Rhode Design
137–139 Essex Road
London N1 2NR
020 7354 9933
Bespoke kitchen makers and showroom of units and accessories

SieMatic
Osprey House
Rookery Court
Primett Road
Stevenage
Hertfordshire SG1 3EE
Smart contemporary kitchens

Leather flooring, walling and furniture

J.T. Batchelor Ltd
9–10 Culford Mews
London N1 4DZ
020 7254 2962
Leather merchants

Alma Home
Unit D, 12–14 Greatorex Street
London E1 5NF
020 7377 0762
www.almahome.co.uk
Leather floor and wall tiles available in a range of skins, plus furniture and home accessories

Bill Amberg
31 Elkstone Road
London W10 5NT
020 8960 2000
www.billamberg.com
Bespoke leather furniture, floor and wall tiles, rugs and accessories

Lighting

Aktiva
10b Spring Place
London NW5 3BH
020 7428 9325
www.aktiva.co.uk
Producer of low-voltage modern light fittings

Alva
4 Ella Mews
Cressy Road
London NW3 2NH
020 7482 4331
www.alvalighting.com
Contemporary lighting

Arc Creations
10 Banchurch Road
Brighton
East Sussex BN2 3PJ
01273 694424
Innovative modern lighting

Aria
295–296 Upper Street
London N1 2TU
020 7704 1999
www.aria-shop.co.uk
Modern interior design shop with lighting

Artemide
92a Great Portland Street
London W1W 7JY
020 7637 7238
www.artemide.com
Renowned Italian lighting designs

Atrium
Centrepoint
22–24 St Giles High Street
London WC2H 8TA
020 7379 7288
www.atrium.ltd.uk
Contemporary interior design and lighting including designs by Ingo Maurer

John Cullen Lighting
585 King's Road
London SW6 2EH
020 7371 5400
www.johncullenlighting.co.uk
Designers and makers of contemporary fittings for all applications

Erco
38 Dover Street
London W1S 4NL
020 7408 0320 (for stockists)
www.erco.com
Leading manufacturers of high-quality light fittings, favoured by architects

Flos
31 Lisson Grove
London NW1 6UB
020 7258 0600
www.flos.net
Contemporary lighting from designers such as Achille Castiglioni, Philippe Starck and Jasper Morrison

Fontana Arte
Available in the UK at
Clementa Cavigioli
Walmer Studios
235–239 Walmer Road
London W11 4EY
020 7792 2522
Classic modern Italian lighting

Mathmos
20–24 Old Street
London EC1V 9AP
020 7549 2700
www.mathmos.co.uk
Famous for the Lava Lamp, but there's more besides

SKK
34 Lexington Street
London W1F 0LH
020 7434 4095
www.skk.net
Contemporary lighting

Metal and metalworkers

PMF Designs
Unit N, Quarry Road
Newhaven
East Sussex BN9 9DG
01273 517333
www.pmfdesigns.co.uk
Contemporary metal furniture for the home or garden in steel, stainless steel, brass or aluminium

Metal flooring

Bragman Flett
Unit 4, 193 Garth Road
Morden
Surrey SM4 4LZ
020 8337 1934
www.bragmanflett.co.uk
Aluminium sheet flooring to specification

Gooding Aluminium
1 British Wharf
Landmann Way
London SE14 5RS
020 8692 2255 (for brochures and samples)
www.goodingalum.com
Aluminium sheet flooring

Natural floorcoverings

Alternative Flooring Co.
Unit 3b, Stephenson Close
East Portway
Andover
Hants SP10 3RU
01264 335111 for stockists
www.alternative-flooring.co.uk
Coir, seagrass, sisal, jute and bespoke rugs

Crucial Trading
79 Westbourne Park Road
London W2 5QH
020 7221 9000
sales@crucial-trading.com
Natural flooring in sisal, coir, rush, jute and even paper

Forbo-Nairn
PO Box 1, Kirkcaldy
Fife KY1 2SB
01592 643777 for stockists
www.marmoleum.co.uk
UK's sole maker of linoleum sheets and tiles

Kersaint Cobb & Co.
Gorsey Lane
Coleshill
Birmingham B46 1JU
01675 430430
www.kersaintcobb.co.uk
Natural floorcoverings, including sisal, coir and New Zealand rugs

Siesta Cork Tiles
Unit 21, Tait Road
Gloucester Road
Croydon
Surrey CR0 2DO
020 8683 4055
www.siestacorktiles.co.uk
Cork products for floors and walls

Natural Flooring
www.naturalflooringdirect.com

Stovax Original Style
Falcon Road
Sowton Industrial Estate
Exeter
Devon EX2 7LF
01392 474011 for brochure
www.stovax.com
Floor and wall tiles

UK Marble
www.ukmarble.co.uk

Office furniture

See also listings under Furniture and home accessories

Chaplins
17–18 Berners Street
London W1T 3LN
020 7323 6552
www.chaplins.co.uk
Large selection of contemporary furniture, including Tisettanta, Emmemobili and Cassina

Paint

Akzo Nobel
www.deco.akzonobel.com
www.crownpaint.co.uk
A wide range of interior and exterior paints, including the Crown brand

C. Brewer & Sons
Albany House
Ashford Road
Eastbourne
East Sussex BN21 3TR
01323 411080
www.brewers.co.uk
Home delivery service for paints and wallpapers

Leyland Paints
Huddersfield Road
Birstall
Batley
West Yorkshire WF15 7LS
01924 354500
www.leyland-paints.co.uk
Colour Matching Service can match a paint to any wallpaper, fabric or other colour swatch

Plastics and acrylics

Baldwin Plastic Laminates
57 Tallon Road
Hutton Industrial Estate
Brentwood
Essex CM13 1TG
01277 225235
Laminated kitchen worktops and surfaces

Stainless steel worktops and splashbacks

GEC Anderson
Oakengrove, Shire Lane
Hastoe
Tring
Hertfordshire, HP23 6LY
01442 826999
www.gecanderson.co.uk
Stainless steel sinks and worktops in any size and shape. Also splashbacks, panels, cabinets, drawer units and sanitary appliances

Link Catering Equipment
10 Greenhey Place
Skelmersdale
Lancashire WN8 9SA
01695 722168

Stone flooring, tiles and worktops

Attica
543 Battersea Park Road
London SW11 3BL
020 7924 7875
www.attica.co.uk
Ceramic, marble and stone

Bisazza UK
020 8640 7994
www.bisazza.it
Ceramic flooring including mosaics

Steve Charles & Co.
The Engineering Offices
2 Michael Road
London SW6 2AD
020 7384 4424
www.stevecharles.com
Unusual ceramics and stone flooring from all over the world

Classical Flagstones
The Old Dairy, Lower Ledge Farm
Dyrham
Chippenham
Wiltshire SN14 8EY
01225 316759
www.classical-flagstones.com
Stone tiles, cobbles and flags

Delabole Slate
Pengelly Road
Delabole
Cornwall PL33 9AZ
01840 212242
www.delaboleslate.com
Slate floor tiles

Hanson Bath and Portland Stone
Monks Park Mine, Monks Lane
Corsham
Wiltshire SN13 9PH
01225 811154
Bath and Portland stone

Hard Rock Flooring
Fleet Marston Farm
Fleet Marston
Aylesbury
Buckinghamshire HP18 0PL
01296 658 755
www.hardrockflooring.co.uk
Natural stone flooring

H&L Marble
15a Wadsworth Road
Greenford
Middlesex UB6 7JN
020 8810 9223
Granite, limestone and marble

Kirkstone
Skelworth Bridge
Nr Ambleside
Cumbria LA22 9NN
01539 433296
www.kirkstone.com
Slate, granite and limestone for floors, walls and worktops

Limestone Gallery
Arch 47, South Lambeth Road
London SW8 1SS
020 7735 8555
Antique and modern stone flooring, UK's largest selection of limestone flooring

Lloyd of Bedwyn
91 Church Street
Great Bedwyn
Marlborough
Wiltshire SN8 3PF
01672 870234
www.lloydofbedwyn.net
All types of stone floor and surfaces

Mediterraneo
Studio C3
The Old Imperial Laundry
71 Warriner Gardens
London SW11 4XW
www.mediterraneodesign.com
Great range of top-quality floor and wall tiles

Paris Ceramics
583 King's Road
London SW6 2EH
020 7371 7778
Vast selection of flooring materials including tiles, stone and mosaics

Slate World
In association with American Slate Co. UK
020 7384 9595
www.slateworld.com
Flooring and paving in a large range of natural colours

Stone Age
19 Filmer Road
London SW6 7BU
020 7385 7954
www.estone.co.uk
www.stone-age.co.uk
Importers of stone from around the world

Stonell
521–525 Battersea Park Road
London SW11 3BN
020 7738 0606
www.stonell.co.uk
A huge variety of real stone flooring

Synthethic floorcoverings

Altro Floors
Works Road
Letchworth
Hertfordshire SG6 1NW
01462 480480 for stockists
www.altro.co.uk
Vinyl, PVC and rubber flooring

Amtico
Epsom Business Park
Kiln Lane
Epsom
Surrey KT17 1DH
01372 745909
www.amtico.com
Maker of a huge range of vinyl flooring

Dalsouple
PO Box 140
Bridgwater
Somerset TA5 1HT
01984 667551 for stockists
www.dalsouple.com
Rubber flooring

Gerflor UK
020 7723 6601 for stockists
Sheet and tile vinyl and rubber flooring

Harvey Maria
Trident Business Centre
89 Bickersteth road
London SW17 9SH
020 8516 7788
www.harveymaria.co.uk
Laminated photographic tiles in patterns of grass, pebbles, leaves and more

Underfloor heating

Floorheatech
Bowen House
Bredgar Road
Gillingham
Kent ME8 6PL
0800 8144328
www.floorheatech.co.uk

Vintage furniture and home accessories

Bentply
Unit G1, Ground Floor
13 Church Street
London NW8
020 8346 1387
www.bentply.com
Classic thirties Modernist furniture

Eat My Handbag Bitch
37 Drury Lane
London WC2B 5RR
020 7836 0830
www.eatmyhandbagbitch.co.uk
Quality post-war furniture, including Italian, British and Scandinavian design

Showhome
www.ourshowhome.com
Specialists in Danish furniture and accessories

Wood flooring, panelling and worktops

Agora London
The Coach House
8 Avenue Crescent
London W3 8EW
020 8752 8648
Antique French oak flooring

English Timbers
1a Main Street
Kirkburn, Driffield
East Yorkshire Y025 9DU
01377 229301
www.englishtimbers.co.uk
Hardwood flooring

Finewood Floors
Suite F5, Skillion Business Centre
1 Hawley Road
London N18 3SB
020 8884 1515
www.finewoodfloors.co.uk
Specialist in all types of hardwood, strip and parquet, in particular wide plank flooring

Hardwood Flooring Co.
146–152 West End Lane
London NW6 1SD
020 7328 8481
www.hardwood-flooring.uk.com
Stockist of Junkers, Kahrs plus reclaimed and new strip, blocks and planks

J. Crispin & Sons
92–96 Curtain Road
London EC2A 3AA
020 7739 4857/2131
Veneer merchants and importers

James Latham plc
Leeside Wharf, Mount Pleasant Hill
London E5 9NG
020 8806 3333
Hardwood, softwood and panel products, including MDF, plywood and veneered panels

LBC Hardwood Flooring
Unit 9, Knutsford Way
Sealand Road Industrial Estate
Chester CH1 4NS
01244 377811
Suppliers and fitters of new and old, plank, strip and block flooring

Liberon Waxes
Mountfield Industrial Estate
Learoyd Road, New Romney
Kent TN28 8XU
01797 367555
Specialist finishes and treatments for wood

Plyboo (UK) Ltd
55–57 Main Street, Alford
Aberdeenshire AB33 8AA
01975 563388
Bamboo flooring and panelling

Perstorp Surface Materials (UK) Ltd
Aycliffe Industrial Park
Newton Aycliffe
Co Durham DL5 6EF
08705 143022
'Pergo' laminate flooring from Sweden

Wooden decking

Outdoor Decking Company UK
www.outdoordeck.co.uk
High-quality, bespoke timber decking

Index

Picture credits

The publisher has made every effort to trace the copyright holders, architects and designers of the pictures used in this book. We apologise in advance of any unintentional omissions and would be pleased to insert the appropriate acknowledgement in any subsequent edition.

2 Photographer Tim Evan-Cook/Red Cover/Designers Marta Pan and André Wogenscky; **4** Photographer Hayo Heye/Schöner Wohnen/Camera Press/Designer Siw Matzen; **11** Photographer Peter Cook/View/Architect Feeny Mallindine Architects; **12 bottom right** Photographer Matthew Donaldson for Cassina; **13** Photographer Åke E:son Lindman/Architect Shideh Shaygan; **14 bottom left** Photographer James Merrell for SCP; **15** Photographer Anthony Cotsifas/Architect Smith-Miller + Hawkinson Architects; **16 top centre and top right** Photographer Mario Carrieri for Cassina; **17** Photographer Craig Hudson/Architect George Elphick at Elphick Proome Architects; **18 top right** Vitra Design Museum; **19** Photographer Åke E:son Lindman/Architect Anna von Schewen Design & Architecture; **21** Photographer Matt Chisnall/Architect Simon Allford at Allford Hall Monaghan Morris; **23** Photographer Åke E:son Lindman/Architect Magnus Ståhl Architect; **24 top right** Vitra Design Museum; **24 bottom left** Vitra Design Museum; **25** Photographer Philip Bier/View/Architect David Bishop at Bluebottle; **26 middle centre** Photographer Aldo Ballo for Cassina; **26 bottom right** Photographer Oliviero Venturi for Cassina; **27** Photographer Richard Glover/View/Architect Pablo Uribe; **29** Photographer Alan Williams/Architect A-EM Architects; **31** Photographer Andreas von Einsiedel/Architect Featherstone Associates; **33** Photographer Peter Cook/View/Architect Fiona Mclean at Mclean Quinlan; **37** Photographer Graham Atkins Hughes for *ELLE Decoration UK*/Architect Denton Corker Marshall Architects; **38 top second right** Photographer Andrea Zani for Cassina; **38 top right** Herman Miller, Inc; **38 centre left** Herman Miller, Inc; **39** Photographer Åke E:son Lindman/Architect Claesson Koivisto Rune; **40 top right** Photographer Andrea Zani for Cassina; **41** Photographer Nicholas Kane/arcaid.co.uk/Architect David Mikhail Architects; **43** Photographer Andreas von Einsiedel/Architect John Crummay & Robin Rout; **44 top left** Photographer Andrea Zani for Cassina; **44 bottom right** Photographer F Obbiettivo for Cassina; **45** Photographer Edmund Sumner/View/Architect Plastik Architects; **46 top right** Photographer Aldo Ballo for Casssina; **47** Photographer Andreas von Einsiedel/Architect Featherstone Associates & Dominic Ash; **49** Photographer Pernille Schlosser/Designer Heine Design; **51** Photographer James Silverman/Architect Wahlström & Steijner Architects; **55** Photographer Jonathan Pile/Architect Project Orange; **57** Photographer James Silverman/Architect Rahel Belatchew Lerdell; **59** Photographer Bertrand Limbour/Camera Press/*Marie Claire Maison*/Architect Etienne van den Berg; **61** Photographer Henry Wilson/Red Cover/Architect Nick McMahon; **63** Photographer Winfried Heinze/Red Cover/Architect Tonkin Liu; **64 top second right** Vitra Design Museum; **65** Architect KSR Architects; **67** Photographer James Winspear/View/Architect Consarc Architects with Bluestone Kitchens; **69** Photographer Dan Tobin Smith/Camera Press/*Marie Claire Maison*/Architect Ann Boyd Design; **71** Photographer Peter Cook/View/Architect Paul Mullins Associates; **73** Photographer Edmund Sumner/View/Architect Ash Sakula Architects; **77** Photographer Graham Atkins Hughes for *ELLE Decoration UK*/Architect Denton Corker Marshall Architects; **79** Photographer Åke E:son Lindman/Architect Claesson Koivisto Rune; **81** Photographer James Silverman/Architect Rahel Belatchew Lerdell; **83** Photographer Jonathan Pile/Architect Project Orange; **85** Photographer James Silverman/Architect Phil Simmons at Simmons Interiors; **87** Photographer Andreas von Einsiedel/Architect Groupe l'Arche with Wessel von Loringhoven at CasaNova; **89** Photographer Philippe Ruault/Architect Jean Nouvel; **91** Photographer Richard Glover/View/Architect Form Design Architecture; **93** Photographer Alexandre Weinberger/Camera Press/Designer Philippe Starck; **95** Photographer Matt Chisnall/Architect Simon Allford at Allford Hall Monaghan Morris; **97** Photographer Mark York/Red Cover/Architect Alison Brooks Architects; **99** Photographer Steve Stephens/Luchford/Architect Fox Linton Associates; **103** Photographer Åke E:son Lindman/Architect Harry Elson Architect; **105** Photographer Richard Bryant/arcaid.co.uk/Architect Terry Farrell & Partners for Berkeley/Designer Tara Bernerd at Target Living; **106 centre right** Product Hang-it-all/Designers Charles & Ray Eames (1953)/Photographer Andreas Sütterlin for Vitra Design Museum; **107** Photographer James Silverman/Architect Rene Dekker; **109** Photographer Richard Glover/View/Architect DSP Architects; **110 bottom right** Photographer Oliviero Venturi for Cassina; **111** Photographer Graham Atkins Hughes for *ELLE Decoration UK*/Furnished by Atomic Interiors (0115 941 5577); **113** Photographer Jonathan Pile/Architect Project Orange; **115** Photographer Chris Gascoigne/View/Architect John Kerr Associates; **117** Photographer Habitat/Red Cover/Architect Marco Bezzoli, Michael Borgstrom & Adi Goren at architecture dot com; **119** Photographer Bo Bedre/Architect Knud Holscher; **120 top left** Photographer Oliviero Venturi for Cassina; **121** Photographer Luke White for *ELLE Decoration UK*/Architect Robert Dye at Robert Dye Associates; **125** Photographer Richard Croft/IPC/*Living etc*/Architect Berthold Lubetkin/Designer Ou Baholyodhin Studio; **127** Photographer Tom Scott/Architect Grut Partnership & Toh Shimazaki Architecture; **128 top left** Photographer Oliviero Venturi for Cassina; **129** Photographer Christian Richters/Architect Francine Houben at Mecanoo; **131** Photographer James Balston/Arcblue/Architect Rainer Spehl; **132 bottom centre** Photographer Bitetto Chimenti for Cassina; **132 bottom right** Photographer Aldo Ballo for Cassina; **133** Photographer Werner Huthmacher/Artur/Architect Augustin + Frank Architekten; **135** Vitsoe Design Service; **137** Photographer Tom Scott/Architect Mary Manatiy at Marston Manatiy Design; **138 centre second right** Herman Miller, Inc; **139** Photographer Mikael Lindén/Architect Haroma Partners; **143** Photographer Clive Nicols Garden Pictures/Designer Nina Thalinson at Lust & Fägring; **145** Photographer Clive Nicols Garden Pictures/Designer Stephen Woodhams; **147** Photographer David Clerihew/IPC/*Living etc*/Designer Karena Batstone Design & Helen Tindale at Reversed Out; **149** Photographer Andreas von Einseidel/Designer Candy and Candy; **151** Photographer Clive Nicols Garden Pictures/Designer Joe Swift and Thamasin Marsh at The Plant Room.

Acknowledgements

First, I would like to thank every architect and designer who has contributed to this book – without your inspiring work this project would have been impossible. I'd also like to thank the team at Quadrille: Alison Cathie, Jane O'Shea and Helen Lewis, editor Lisa Pendreigh for her inexhaustible enthusiasm and scrupulous attention to detail, picture researcher Helen Stallion for scouring the globe for fantastic projects, and, of course, designers Ros Holder and Sue Storey for a great looking book that we can all be proud of.

page 2 Saint Rémy home of sculptor Martha Pan and architect André Wogensky with classic Series 7 chairs in black by Arne Jacobsen.
page 4 Tranquil interior in neutral stone and white colours with a courageous aubergine-coloured wall mural of the desert by Hamburg designer Siw Matzen.

Editorial Director Jane O'Shea
Creative Director Helen Lewis
Project Editor Lisa Pendreigh
Designers Ros Holder and Sue Storey
Picture Researcher Helen Stallion
Production Director Vincent Smith
Production Controller Rebecca Short

First published in 2004 by
Quadrille Publishing Limited
Alhambra House
27–31 Charing Cross Road
London WC2H 0LS

Text © Fay Sweet 2004
Design and layout © Quadrille Publishing Limited 2004

British Library Cataloguing-in-Publication Data
A catalogue record for this book is available from the British Library.

ISBN 1-84400-120-2

Printed in China

The publisher has made every effort to ensure the website information given in this book is correct. Any changes to website addresses are not the responsibility of the publisher.